D0867871

the Politics of God
and
the Politics of Man

Books by Jacques Ellul Available in English

The Theological Foundation of Law (1960; 1969)
The Technological Society (1964)
Propaganda (1966)
The Political Illusion (1967)
The Presence of the Kingdom (1967)
A Critique of the New Commonplaces (1968)
Violence: Reflections from a Christian Perspective (1969)
To Will and To Do (1969)
The Meaning of the City (1970)
Prayer and Modern Man (1970)
The Judgment of Jonah (1971)
The Politics of God and the Politics of Man (1972)

the Politics of God
and
the Politics of Man

by

JACQUES ELLUL

translated and edited by

GEOFFREY W. BROMILEY

William B. Eerdmans Publishing Company
Grand Rapids, Michigan

Copyright © 1972 by William B. Eerdmans Publishing Company
All rights reserved
Library of Congress Catalog Card Number: 76-188247
ISBN 0-8028-1442-5
Printed in the United States of America

Third printing, May 1977

Translated from the French *Politique de Dieu, politiques de l'homme,* Nouvelle alliance, Editions Universitaires, Paris, 1966

Translator's Preface

This new study by Jacques Ellul follows the customary pattern of the author. It is not an academic work in the accepted sense. Although based on biblical passages, it is not a scientific commentary. Nor does it consist of political, sociological, or economic analysis. Nor is it theological in the sense of rigorous dogmatic enquiry. It simply consists of readings and meditations in the Second Book of Kings with a concluding meditation on inutility.

Yet the form of the book, as in the case of the author's other writings, should not cause us to dismiss it as of little consequence. In his allusive way Ellul is in fact one of the most important and penetrating thinkers of our time, and it is doubtful whether any academic work could present a more authentically radical discussion of theology and politics than what we have with such deceptive simplicity in these pages.

Ellul raises question after question with an eye always on the modern scene. Can we fulfil the plan and purpose of God by political means? Is it possible to fulfil God's aim and yet to sin against God and incur his judgment? Are we in danger of getting out of our depth when we plunge into social action? Does the world really take us as seriously as we take ourselves in such matters? May there be a time when withdrawal is more effective than action? What is the real nature of a prophetic ministry?

Theological issues, which can throw a searching light on modern values, are also raised. There is the problem of miracles. This merges into the broader problem of the interrelation of divine and human purpose and action. This

5

in turn leads us to the problem of efficacy or success and the question whether our greatest sin today, not least in the church, is to measure acts by their usefulness when what is really needed is a qualitative criterion.

One might almost say that Ellul's work, although he himself would probably reject the description, has a genuinely prophetic dimension. The form is artless, concealing rather than revealing the great resources of learning, thought, and experience which underlie it. But for seeing eyes and hearing ears this is a profound and searching work which, if it is heeded, might well recall the church to a better assessment of itself and a truer understanding of its mission and ministry.

Geoffrey W. Bromiley

Pasadena, California

Contents

Introduction

All the stories we shall read are set in the perspective of Jesus Christ. It is impossible to ignore the fact of the unity of revelation and its movement. Everything leads to Jesus Christ, just as everything comes from him. Hence Jesus Christ is not absent from the somber adventure of the Second Book of Kings. It also seems to be equally impossible to ignore at the commencement of these meditations the one in the narratives in whom we are to see a figure of Jesus Christ, namely, Elisha. It is true that some of the texts of Kings on which we shall be meditating refer to the period after Elisha's death (2 Kings 16-18). Nevertheless he is still the decisive personage, and the orientation of the later stories is fixed by him.[1]

Elijah is traditionally represented as the one who will return, and whose return will intimate the end of times. He did not die but was transported to heaven, and he will return from thence in the last days. In Malachi 3-4, God declares that it is he who will be the herald of the Lord's coming. Expectation of his return was so certain that those who saw Christ's passion thought he was calling on Elijah.

Elijah is the one who precedes the Lord, and Jesus confirms that he has come already when he says that John the Baptist is the returned Elijah. But "they did to him whatever they pleased . . . " (Matthew 17:12). If, however, Elijah precedes the Lord as John the Baptist precedes Jesus, then one must admit that Elisha is a figure, a living

---

[1] Note that in what follows we are simply repeating what W. Vischer has pointed out already.

9

prophecy, a type of Jesus Christ, the more so as Elijah describes him in the same way as John describes Jesus, namely, as the one who is to come. It should also be noted that the names of Jesus and Elisha have the same meaning—God helps, or God has helped—and it is common knowledge how very important was the signification of the names people bore in Israel. Furthermore, Elisha is called much greater than Elijah; he received a double portion of the spirit that animated Elijah. Nor does this double portion come to him as the personal gift or grant of Elijah; it comes through God's miraculous intervention. Because he has seen the chariot of fire of the Eternal, he knows that in fulfilment of Elijah's prophecy he has received a double portion of the Spirit. And this proclamation of Elisha's power takes place on the banks of the Jordan. From this moment there is found what might be called the explosive presence of the Spirit. The prophetic ministry of Elisha is characterized by an abundance of miracles which it is hard to credit. These miracles are of every order, quality, and dimension. We are often restive, full of doubts, and ill at ease in face of these miracles of Elisha, which often seem to be miracles of poor quality to Christian piety: children torn to pieces by bears; the head of the axe floating; the healing of the inedible pottage. We find it hard to see the meaning or value of these miracles of the Eternal.

Often they look like pure and simple acts of magic, and we are inclined to dismiss Elisha as a mere wonder-worker. But can we forget that some of the miracles of Jesus also seem to have a magical aspect, for example, the clay mixed to cure the blind man, or the healing of the woman by simply touching the garment of Jesus?

This is not enough to demote Elisha from his role as a type of Jesus Christ. Indeed, should we not compare some of the miracles performed by the two, for example, the multiplication of the loaves in almost exactly the same terms ("Give ye them to eat"), and the raising of the son of the Shunammite widow at the very same place where Jesus raised the son of the widow of Nain? There is more than chance here.

As in the case of Jesus, the point of the superabundance of miracles is simply to indicate the unbounded presence of the Spirit.

But another aspect of Elisha also disturbs us. This is his political role. He is closely involved in the political life of his day. He changes it, as we shall see. And his role differs from that of Elijah.

The mission of Elijah was to maintain the purity of the religion of the Eternal, the holiness of God. He had to fight against all adulteration. He had to bring Israel back to loyalty and to destroy idolatry. In a sense this was also the mission of John the Baptist with his baptism of repentance and purification. And this is also why it is said of Elijah that he will restore all things. But the task or vocation of Elisha is very different. He is a prophet, not of purity, but of power. He affirms that God is King. His acts and interventions signify the universality and the proximity of the kingdom of God. The kingdom of God has drawn near, completely changes political life like everything else, and manifests itself by this outburst of miracles of all kinds, political included. God is the God of all peoples. He reigns over all kings. He directs world politics. These are the points to which the miracles of Elisha bear witness. This is the concrete significance and material expression of the lordship of God. When we are told that the kingdom is at hand, this has a political sense too, and the political sense is the one which Elisha brings out. Like all the prophets of Jesus Christ, he indicates and bears witness only to a second and relative aspect of what Jesus Christ will be and do. Nevertheless, this is also contained in the total revelation given in Jesus Christ.

Might one also suggest that if it was asked of Jesus: "Can anything good come out of Nazareth?" (John 1:46),

11

one should remember that in the days of Elisha Galilee belonged to the Northern Kingdom and Elisha was the prophet of this kingdom?

We shall not insist further on this feature of Elisha, but we would have the reader keep in mind constantly as he meditates on these texts that Elisha is an image of Christ; in this light order and signification are given to everything else. It is not, however, the aim of the present study to show this.

Each book of Scripture has its own particular sense, emphasis, and perspective. Each reflects one aspect of God's total revelation. Each imparts a unique and singular truth. Yet they cannot be rigorously separated from one another. On the other hand, they are not to be confused with one another. Each has its special character. We are not just to draw out the main lines. This would be of no particular value in the Bible. Naturally everything is in everything. But it seems to me that the idea of finding everything in every text serves no useful purpose.[2]

---

[2] We are not pretending here to give a full commentary on the Second Book of Kings. We are simply choosing out certain types according to what seems to us to be the unique and decisive orientation of this book, according to the intention which it seems one can gather from it.

We are not pretending to be doing scientific work. There will be no minute exegesis nor division of the work into strata according to probable dates of composition.

There will be no attempt to discover what stage the book represents in the spiritual history of Israel nor why it was written at this period in political history. Neither the forms nor the spirit of form criticism will be adopted. Such are now the usual objects of biblical science. We shall not ignore them, but in our view these inner researches, though they are of value, are definitely restricted in scope, and only very relatively offer a deeper exposition of the text of the Bible. We shall adopt the simple attitude of the believer with his Bible who through the text that he reads is ultimately trying to discover what is the Word of God, and what is the final meaning of his life in the presence of this text.

We are at the level of the kind of meditation which does not seem to be any the less important exegetically because it is not scientific.

If we have, of course, certain hermeneutical presuppositions, this is not the place to defend them. They are at least as well founded as those of different schools.

We believe that every book of Scripture should be taken for what it purports to be. This is the first principle of interpretation. In any biblical writing we can readily see other things than what it seems to be, but these ought to be secondary and relatively unimportant compared to what the writing itself says it is and seeks to be. For it is perhaps there that we shall find the meaning that God intends us to see in this work. Or, very explicitly, this Second Book of Kings describes for us God's interventions in a period in the history of the kingdoms of Judah and Israel.

It seems to me, then, that this Second Book of Kings is characterized by two aspects of revelation. The first is political in the narrow sense; the problems in most of the texts are political. The problem is Israel's situation as regards political power in relation to the Syrians, the Assyrians, the Edomites, and the Egyptians. It is Israel's decadence as a kingdom. And we shall see directly the place, the presence, and the action of God in this area of human life.

The Second Book of Kings is probably the most political of all the books of the Bible. For its reference is to Israel genuinely constituted as a political power and playing its part in the concert of empires. Furthermore, its reference is also to an age of crisis. Above all, we see here politics in action and not just in principle. We see ethical or spiritual orientations as in Paul's Epistles.

All this is not unimportant in face of those who think the political problem should not be discussed in the church. The Bible shows us that the church is not just a spiritual matter, that politics is not just simply a human action of no concern to us. It may be that politics is the kingdom of the devil, but this certainly concerns us as Christians.

This meditation is also not unimportant in face of those who want politics to be the main action of men, and of

13

Christians who think involvement in politics is essential and for whom everything is finally politics.

In fact these texts show the relativity of politics, which is the sphere of the greatest affirmation of man's autonomy, of his revolt, of his pretentious attempt to play the role of God. And willingly or not God steps in again. Now politics raises a special problem. In Christian circles there has often been reference to the doctrine of the state. The theology of government is well known and has been much debated. But there is a world of difference between the state and political action. To recognize the legitimacy of power and the validity of authority does not imply at all that one does the same in relation to politics; I am using the term here in the most realistic sense. It is simply to take part in a collective movement which talks of politics and which is found at the popular level. We are in the world of the political illusion which is of neither value nor interest. If it is a question of divinely ordained submission in an attitude of explicitly Christian debate and wrestling of conscience, we have here an important function in relation to the state but we are not engaged in politics. Karl Barth himself confuses the state and politics when he says that since Christians recognize in the order of the sword, of constraint, and of fear a divine dispensation, they cannot be antipolitical or apolitical.

The real problem is that of active participation in real political action, that is, the discharge of a directive function in a party or a state organism. In this alone one is engaged in politics; the rest is a matter of opinion, obedience, or debate, but it is in no sense politics. Now the problem that is posed in the Second Book of Kings is exclusively the problem of political action and not that of the state.

It is from this first perspective of politics that we shall select our texts, although we shall certainly not forget that Elisha's work is a close intermingling of political action

14

and the individual witness of love. Between his actions in relation to Moab and Naaman come the miracle of the oil and that of the raising of the small child. Between the siege of Samaria and the drama of Hazael comes the act of justice on behalf of the disinherited woman. This close intermingling of the public and the individual is the specific testimony of the prophet Elisha. Our present concern, however, is only with his political action.

Now it must also be understood that there is no question here of trying to arrive at a politics taken from Holy Scripture. One might even say that the very reverse is the case.

In these stories we shall see an intervention by God in political action as men devise and pursue it. The order is that of history and not of principles. We shall also see God's judgment on politics. The order is that of prophecy and revelation, not of ethics and political procedures.

This introduces us to a second aspect of the Second Book of Kings, to its specific revelation. More than anything else, it seems to me, it displays concretely the play of what Karl Barth has called the free determination of man in the free decision of God. We are constantly in the presence of the relation between man's action and God's. The trend of history in political situations brings us to one of those *cruces theologiae* well known in metaphysics and rationally insoluble. If God is omnipotent, he cannot allow man any freedom, and man, when he acts, can only execute mechanically what God has ordained. On the other hand, if man has freedom, if he makes his own decisions, God is simply a theoretical, abstract, or impotent God. Now in the present stories this academic problem is certainly not resolved in global or intellectual fashion. Rather, it is transported into living reality which cannot possibly be schematized. This is why it is so important to keep the stories as they are. On the one hand we must firmly refuse to make of them a contingent illustration of a doctrine of

15

God. On the other hand we must not make of them a simple historical record, the object of external exegesis and dull science. We are in the presence of life itself at its most profound and most significant. We must not let it slip away from us. At every point we shall see the affirmation of a divine will, but it never acts directly. It transmits, expresses, and executes itself through human intermediaries. These do not have to be Israelites, believers, the righteous. God also acts through others.

Furthermore, this divine will never constrains man directly to execute literally what it represents. We are in the presence of a kind of proposition or project which God makes known with full respect for the independence of man.

God does not mechanize man. He gives him free play. He includes issues of every possible kind. Man is at the time independent. We cannot say free. Scripture everywhere reminds us that man's independence in relation to God is in the strict sense bondage as regards sin. This man is not free. He is under the burden of his body and his passions, the conditioning of society, culture, and function. He obeys its judgments and setting. He is controlled by its situation and psychology. Man is certainly not free in any degree. He is the slave of everything save God. God does not control or constrain him. God lets him remain independent in these conditions.

And these are the conditions which the Second Book of Kings describes for us very practically in each incident. We see man deciding on a great number of actions freely and alone. Many of them fail. They are nonsensical. They misfire. They are lost in the sand. But some succeed. And when this occurs, these deliberate acts which men do for their own reasons and according to their own calculations are the very ones which accomplish just what God had decided and was expecting (even though the men often do not know this or are not aware of it at first). These acts enter into God's design and bring about exactly the new situation which God planned.

But in this relation between God's decision and man's we must not be content with too simple a schema, for we sometimes see in the stories that none of man's decisions enters into God's project, that none of the choices he makes in his independence is able to advance the situation or achieve God's plan. Man can create new situations which God did not will. And since the Lord does not give up, i.e., does not give up doing not his tyrannical will, but what is good for man and man's salvation, he changes his plans, accepts the new situation and enters into it, and he draws from it certain consequences which man certainly did not expect or foresee but which will finally work for the actualizing of God's love.

For if God's ways are higher than our ways, we must also remember, as Ephesians 3:10 tells us, that his wisdom is multiple, that is, the modalities of his government are without number.

Although it does not fall within our text, we may recall the most familiar example of what we have just said, namely, the establishment of the monarchy in Israel. The chosen people feels the sociological pressure of neighboring peoples. All nations have a certain type of government, namely, monarchy.

From a human standpoint Israel feels that monarchy would be an organizational advance, that it is both more efficient and more secure, that it allows of political planning in a way that the system of the judges did not. All this is at the level of political judgment and it leaves out of account the fact that the prior regime was divinely given. From the standpoint of political efficiency Israel was undoubtedly right.

Sociologically monarchy is an advance on a feudal or tribal system. Israel takes the most advanced nations as its model. It wants to assimilate itself to them. But God does not want this form of government, for it will introduce confusion between Yahweh and his "incarnation" in the king. God objects, but Israel insists, demanding this reasonable advance. So God warns his people. We are given an extraordinary description of what centralized political power inevitably means: more taxes, military conscription, arbitrary police, the impossibility of limiting power. This is the price the people will have to pay to have efficient political power and to reach the level of progress of other nations (for is it not inadmissible that God's people should be the most retrograde and should be the representative of antiquated political structures?). In spite of the divine warning the people is obstinate. It will not accept this warning as a prophecy but treats it as an idle threat. Looking at other peoples, it sees on good evidence the excellence of a glorious king and centralized power. Hence God does not press the point. He accepts this disobedience. He says to the judge: "They have not rejected you, but they have rejected me" (1 Samuel 8:7). We need to catch the pain of God, his mortal suffering, in this simple phrase when he relieves his servant of the wound of being rejected by his people, takes it on himself, and bears the burden of being the God who is rejected by the man he had chosen and loved. But still God does not give up. He does not give up saving the people in spite of itself. He does not give up remedying the progressivist infatuation of this people. Israel wants a king? Even at the cost of rejecting God? Even at the cost of being enslaved? Very well then! God will not oblige or force it to remain in the existing situation.

God will turn to account the new situation created by the stiff-necked independence of the people.

The first king, then, will be Saul, but to show clearly what monarchy really is this king will finally be rejected by God. The second will be David, and so God uses the disobedience of Israel to fashion out of the result of the

18

rebellion the sign, the prophecy, and the ancestor of the one who will come to fulfil all obedience. We see here the mysterious strategy or adaptation of God, and we shall find this again and again in the Second Book of Kings.

But again and inversely, if God finally accomplishes his purpose at the heart of our disobedience, we must also acknowledge the opposite situation, which is no less troubling. The very fact of fulfilling God's will, of entering into his project, of doing what he wants, is no guarantee that God will approve of us and save us and bless us.

Because we do in the political order, in the world's administration, what is needed in God's plan, this does not constitute a claim we can use in God's presence. The man who acts thus may be condemned temporally just because he has done what God expected of him. And this man, or a people, becomes God's instrument and cannot not do what God required. Nevertheless, they are rejected for having done it, perhaps because the domain of politics is also a domain of Satan. Let us turn again to an example outside our own book, namely, in Isaiah 10-11. Because Israel has passed all bounds, because it has been guilty of monstrous injustice, oppressing the poor and exalting its pride without limit, God punishes it. The Assyrian is the rod of his anger: "I command him, to take spoil and seize plunder, and to tread them down like the mire of the streets" (Isaiah 10:6). And this is just what the Assyrian does. Yet this Assyrian does not see that he is an instrument in the hands of the Lord (how could he see it?). This Assyrian has a mind only (v. 7) "to destroy, and to cut off nations not a few" (and why not, since this is just what God sent him to do?). This Assyrian thinks his king is the king of the gods since he has destroyed the nations that trusted in their gods, including the people of Israel. This Assyrian has not understood that although Israel could be treated like Syria or Egypt, yet the God of Israel is very different from the gods of Egypt and Syria. And God gives him time to do all

19

his work. But when this is done, God will judge him too. "Under his glory a burning will be kindled" (v. 16). Certainly the Assyrian will understand none of this. He will no more understand why he collapses than he understood why he achieved universal domination. He will become the very essence of weakness. He will be consumed body and soul. And Israel? A small remnant of Israel will remain, and from this remnant will come the shoot of Jesse in the midst of destruction. This will be at one and the same time both the promise and the fulfilment. At this moment peace and justice and truth will all reign. And the end of this adventure will be that "him shall the nations seek," Assyria included (Isaiah 11:10f.).

This is why we referred to temporal rejection. The Assyrian will be punished in time and history for having devastated Israel and boasting of it, for not having understood the true meaning of its historical enterprise, for having finally obeyed God's will without knowing it was obeying. But he is not damned eternally; he, too, is saved by Christ.

We thus see how complex this relation between man's independence and God's liberty can be. To be sure, during the course of events, when political decisions must be taken, man does not recognize in advance whether or not he is entering into God's plan. What comes out constantly in these stories is that the preliminary question of knowing what is God's will in advance is not the question put by the man of action, by the politician. In the moment of action man follows his own reasons, and this is legitimate. Only afterwards, when the action has been carried out and produced its results, can one see that God's action was done through it, or was not done. There is thus nothing automatic about it. Man chooses his own action. But between this decision by man and God's decision we find the prophet. This man has received a revelation of God's intention either before or during the course of the enterprise. He announces and can bend or provoke, but there is no necessity or determination. One is in the presence of open possibilities here. This man also understands what the politician is wanting. He understands it in depth. He sees the reality behind the appearance of the action, and he discloses to the politician his true intention, his situation.

Finally this man gives the meaning of it all, the true significance of what has happened. He brings to light the relation that exists between the free determination of man and the free decision of God.

Thus the prophet plays a role which is radical and decisive and yet also independent, ex-centric, and disinterested.

In this schematic description of the special features of the Second Book of Kings we see that God does not express his will to us, nor what he has decided to do, in a way which is theoretical, general, and abstract, or, in a word, theological. He acts in the unique course of human lives, of the history of nations, of the pretensions of political powers. He acts, and it is his action itself which is the Word of God. But because this action is not clear, perspicuous, and without ambiguity, because it allows for man's independence, the action of God has to be explained.

We have to demonstrate it to man. We have to put it into language, theory, and theology. There is no other option. The action of God can be grasped indirectly only by the unique one to whom God reveals and declares it himself. This unique one is *the* prophet. He alone knows there is an action of God there. He alone is divinely qualified to declare it. He, then, must explain it. He must engage in the translation into language with all the risks this involves. But at the same time this translation conforms strictly to God's intention, for it is this which preserves for God's action its respectful and noncompulsive character as regards man.

When God himself appears and speaks, whether to Moses, Isaiah, or Paul, there can no longer be any question of autonomy, independence, or liberty on man's part. This is why this mode is rare. When God's act is translated into human words, the hearer can always contest it. He can always declare: This is a myth, an error, an invention, a prophecy *post eventum.*

We discern here an aspect of God's wisdom, of his art of governing the world, the divine action which is made up of respect for man, of finesse, of subtlety, of pedagogy, of choice, of successive adaptations. Yet all this is also inserted into God's omniscience and omnipotence which has prepared everything in advance no matter what may be the solution that each man finally adopts, that God leaves each man free to adopt.

Thus God's action in politics will continually have for us the appearance of vocation, appeal, and address, and then judgment, outburst, and wrath.

It will continually have for us the appearance of grace, of timid approach, of liberation, then of rigor, of inflexibility in attaining its specific end, and sometimes, if rarely, of a miracle which intervenes to overthrow the course of events, of history, and of life.

But in each instance the miracle is related to the man, to the man of God. It does not fall down directly from the sky. It is inserted into the nexus of human actions. It does not have a significance all its own. At the commencement of the miracle the man is associated with it by prayer, and at the conclusion of the miracle he is associated with it by witness and explication. This testimony to the immense love of God which not only creates and saves but which also in its incomprehensible humility wants to associate man with its work, is what is finally set before us from the political standpoint by the Second Book of Kings. This is a remarkable illustration of the fine formula of Pascal that "God has established prayer to communicate the dignity of causality to his creatures."

I

Naaman

2 Kings 5:1-19

1 Naaman, commander of the army of the king of Syria, was a great man with his master and in high favor, because by him the Lord had given victory to Syria. He was a mighty man of valor, but he was a leper. 2 Now the Syrians on one of their raids had carried off a little maid from the land of Israel, and she waited on Naaman's wife. 3 She said to her mistress, "Would that my lord were with the prophet who is in Samaria! He would cure him of his leprosy." 4 So Naaman went in and told his lord, "Thus and so spoke the maiden from the land of Israel." 5 And the king of Syria said, "Go now, and I will send a letter to the king of Israel."

So he went, taking with him ten talents of silver, six thousand shekels of gold, and ten festal garments. 6 And he brought the letter to the king of Israel, which read, "When this letter reaches you, know that I have sent to you Naaman my servant, that you may cure him of his leprosy." 7 And when the king of Israel read the letter, he rent his clothes and said, "Am I God, to kill and to make alive, that this man sends word to me to cure a man of his leprosy? Only consider, and see how he is seeking a quarrel with me."

8 But when Elisha the man of God heard that the king of Israel had rent his clothes, he sent to the king, saying, "Why have you rent your clothes? Let him now come to me, that he may know that there is a prophet in Israel." 9 So Naaman came with his horses and chariots, and halted at the door of Elisha's house. 10 And Elisha sent a messenger to him, saying, "Go and wash in the Jordan seven times, and your flesh shall be restored, and you shall be clean." 11 But Naaman was angry, and went away, saying, "Behold, I thought that he would surely come out to me, and stand, and call on the name of the Lord his God, and wave his hand over the place, and cure the leper. 12 Are not Abana and Pharpar, the rivers of Damascus, better than all the waters of Israel? Could I not wash in them, and be

23

clean?" So he turned, and went away in a rage. 13 But his servants came near and said to him, "My father, if the prophet had commanded you to do some great thing, would you not have done it? How much rather, then, when he says to you, 'Wash, and be clean'?" 14 So he went down and dipped himself seven times in the Jordan, according to the word of the man of God; and his flesh was restored like the flesh of a little child, and he was clean.

15 Then he returned to the man of God, he and all his company, and he came and stood before him; and he said, "Behold, I know that there is no God in all the earth but in Israel; so accept now a present from your servant." 16 But he said, "As the Lord lives, whom I serve, I will receive none." And he urged him to take it, but he refused. 17 Then Naaman said, "If not, I pray you, let there be given to your servant two mules' burden of earth; for henceforth your servant will not offer burnt offering or sacrifice to any God but the Lord. 18 In this matter may the Lord pardon your servant: when my master goes into the house of Rimmon to worship there, leaning on my arm, and I bow myself in the house of Rimmon, when I bow myself in the house of Rimmon, the Lord pardon your servant in this matter." 19 He said to him, "Go in peace."

This is unquestionably one of the best-known stories in the book. The healing of the leper is full of many different lessons both as regards the omnipotence and love of God and also as a prophecy of the healings of Christ. Nevertheless, it seems to us that the text has many aspects which are often neglected and that in the last resort it forces us to raise more questions than it helps us to answer.

In the first instance, and with a reference to the saying of Jesus himself, this miracle is surprising inasmuch as it is not a pure and simple manifestation of God's pity for the sick man. This is not the point. Jesus tells us: 'And there were many lepers in Israel in the time of the prophet Elisha; and none of them was cleansed, only Naaman the Syrian" (Luke 4:27). In another story we shall come across some of those lepers in Israel who were not cured. It is not because the leper is in a sorry state that Naaman is healed. This is not one of the miracles of God's love which is a sign of the restoration of all things in the kingdom.

The miracle has another dimension for Naaman. It has a different orientation. Everything in it astonishes us. Naaman is a general. In spite of the meaning of his name, he is a man of war, a man of blood. Pacifists and proponents of nonviolence have to understand that the man of blood is not excluded from the love of God. Yet our first reaction is necessarily unfavorable. He has chosen violence. Is it not normal, then, that he should be smitten and that he should bear upon himself this uncleanness, the mark of his sin, the sign of his violence?

But Naaman is not only a man of war. He is also a mighty man. He is the king's confidant, the premier. And we know so well that God loves the humble, the poor, and the weak.

We have now seen clearly that the gospel is for the sick, that Jesus makes himself poor among the poor. We know by heart: A curse on your riches. We see only this aspect of God's judgment, that he exalts the humble and abases the proud. Other ages have confused social and political elevation (or success) with God's blessing and with excellence before him. They have known the alliance of throne and altar. To them it would have seemed normal that God should in effect be concerned about this powerful Naaman and that he should cure him . . . in order that he might continue to fulfil his eminent role.

This is no longer the case today. We think the leprosy is simply an expression of the threat: A curse on your riches.

Again, this Naaman is a Syrian. At that time this did not just mean that he was a foreigner. It meant that he was a representative of the power which was perpetually hostile and which was then the most menacing for the kingdom of Israel, having already invaded it several times. Naaman, as a Syrian general, had undoubtedly participated already in the wars against Israel, for we are told that he was an outstanding soldier. This is the man to whom God will manifest his love. Let us recall once more that this is not unique in Scripture. Let us also recall the constant misunderstanding of the gospel we hear today when there is reference to publicans and harlots. Sentimentality has it that these are poor people. Publicans are portrayed as little people and harlots as the miserable prostitutes found on the sidewalks of our big towns. On the other hand the Pharisees are supposedly rich bourgeois. But the historical reality was the exact opposite. The Pharisees were poor enough and they strained their resources by alms and sacrifices. The publicans belonged to great capitalist corporations and were either capitalists themselves or highly paid executives. The harlots were more like the "mondaines" of 1900, i.e., very rich women. Their misery was not at the level of money or social position, which was high, but at the level of contempt. They were despised by those who were really the honest poor and who knew that God is with the poor. They were despised by patriotic Israelites (for these publicans were collaborators with the invader, with the enemy of the chosen people) and by those who upheld the moral standards God had taught his people.

I am sad to say that if we relate this period to a French experience which is just fading, that of 1944-1945, the publicans and harlots around Jesus correspond in some sense to dealers in the black market, to collaborators, and to the women whose hair was sheared off at the liberation. They were that part of the people of Israel which had power through wealth and influence but which was rejected, disdained, and hated by those who were faithful. God constantly reverses our judgments and impulses.

Incidentally the text shows us that this Naaman was in his military function a servant of the Lord whom he did not know. It was by him that the Eternal had delivered the Syrians. This is a strange statement if one takes it seriously. It is an affirmation of Yahweh's universal rule. It is over-facile to evade the difficulty by saying that this is a verse written at the time when Israel was beginning to realize that its God was the God of the whole earth. The point of the incident is to give prominence to this theological affirmation and also to give prominence to the superiority of the people of Israel over all other peoples. Here is an explanation which is no explanation. For one thing, the reference is to the enemy. How could it be admitted that God has as much concern and affection for these Syrians, the constant threat and hereditary enemy, as he does for the Jews themselves? God's interest in this people is truly odd. Again, whether we like it or not, the incident has now been inserted in the book which was accepted by God's people as God's Word. We cannot view it as a stage in the theological elaboration of the concept of God by Israel. We shall continually return to this problem. Either Israel is the chosen people and receives a revelation from God, so that what it holds, transcribes, and transmits is a Word of God and not its own ideas, or Israel is not the chosen people and its ideas and myths and writings are of no more interest than those of the Aztecs or the Japanese.

We have to make a decision here, a decision of faith. For my part I confess that Israel is the chosen people. When, therefore, it holds that God delivered Syria by Naaman, this is not a stage in its own religious evolution; it is the truth of God. Evidently we shall receive no further light on the motives of God in willing this.

Why does God act in favor of the Syrians? There is no point in mentioning the reasons we usually adduce. It is not for the sake of justice. It is not in the name of Syrian independence; the right of national self-determination does not exist in the Bible. Before God nations have neither a right to exist nor a right to liberty. They have no assurance of perpetuity. On the contrary, the lesson of the Bible seems to be that nations are swept away like dead leaves and that occasionally, almost by accident, one might endure rather longer. We do not need to search further. God willed that the Syrians should be delivered, probably from the Assyrians, and he chose a servant to do it, Naaman.

Historical events, then, are basically incomprehensible even though historians can superficially link together causes and effects. The only sure point is that the clearer our understanding is, the more superficial and artificial is the explanation. All the text tells us is that there is an express will of God in historical events for every people, whether it is a believing people or not. But this does not mean in the least that in some evident way historical events are a plain figure of the will of God, as, for example, in *Gesta Dei per Francos,* or Bossuet's *Explication de l'Histoire Universelle.* We must resolutely resist any such idea, even though we may find it again today in the formulae of modern theologians: "Historical events express a Word of God to the church," or: "Christ lives in history."

On the contrary, we must insist on the complete liberty of God and the mysterious character of history. On the one hand we find manifest interventions and declarations between power and power which are in no way related to the will of God. On the other hand we discover invisible, humble interventions which are just the ones that God uses. The king of Syria stands by his general. If there is a chance of curing him it must be taken, and since the healer lives in the kingdom of Samaria, to whom should a king write except to another king? The letter of the king of Syria, and similarly the reaction of the king of Israel, tells us a great deal about the relation between the two peoples. It is obvious that the king of Syria is the stronger. He is of higher rank. He gives the orders. This king of Syria acts like a normal pagan ruler. He believes in magic. In his own land it is the king who controls magical power for the whole people, since he is the divine king. He assumes that the same is true in Israel, and he thus asks his equivalent directly for the miracle.

Again, for one who holds secular power, the other relations are power relations, and the king makes the mistake of the normal politician; he turns to a politician to solve a problem. Now the king of Israel, when he receives the letter, reacts just like the king of Syria. He interprets the act of the latter on the political level. It is strange to note that in the last resort the king of Israel, of all those involved, shows the least faith and the least obedience to the will of God. He acts with reasonable doubt. To be sure, he knows Elisha. He has already had dealings with him. But all the same he does not believe in him. It seems most unlikely to him that the king of Syria has really come seeking a miracle. At the political level such a request can only be a provocation. The whole thing is a disaster. The king of Syria wants a new pretext for war. He is thus asking the impossible. The king of Israel never even thinks of Elisha. After all, who is king? Who holds titular power? Who is in fact the Lord's anointed? Himself. Again we have the self-contemplation of political power which thinks that everything should be arranged at the political level by political means, and that everything has political signification.

The text teaches us that everything does not have to have a political signification and that everything is not necessarily a concern of political powers. At all events we see clearly that it is not by their mediation that God is going to act. The intervention of institutional power is of no interest to God. We have here human actions and reactions that are of no significance. But there is still another character who comes within the sector of powers. This is Naaman himself. He is a mighty man in his own rank from the world's standpoint. He is obeyed and respected. He thinks the prophet will be honored by his visit. Again, he has his own conception of what magicians are like. He has seen them at work in his own land and he expects the same kind of operation. As a man of the world Naaman can allow that the power of one magician may be quantitatively different from that of another. But he can see no qualitative difference. It is always thus in the presence of God. We can grant that he is more powerful, more merciful, etc. But we cannot think of him as quite other than the gods of the world to which we are accustomed.

Naaman, then, is angry because he is not shown due respect, because he is mocked, because he has not been politely treated, and because the man of God has not acted as every proper magician ought to act. Naaman belongs to the secular order. He doubts, and he has reason to doubt, since what is asked of him is in effect absurd. According to his situation, according to his intelligence, and according to his experience, the saying of Elisha is worthless.

It is always thus when the Word of God comes to us. *A priori* it necessarily seems to be absurd, for it is of a different order. And our conversion does not consist in assimilating this Word so that it becomes reasonable. The absurd element persists, but from this moment what becomes absurd is the world, its wisdom, its intelligence, its power, its politics, its experience. For the foolishness of God is wiser than the wisdom of men. After Naaman's conversion what will seem absurd and ridiculous to him will be the manners, the customs, and the religion of Syria.

In comparison with all the decisions and reactions of man which God does not use, which he leaves on one side, we must consider the modest and humble means which God does choose to achieve his purpose. First there is a little girl from the land of Israel who is a slave at Damascus in the household of Naaman. (This proves that there had been earlier wars and that Naaman had had a part in them.) She is the first of God's instruments, a girl (and we know how unimportant women were at this time), a child, a slave. It would be hard to find a more commonplace starting-point or one of less significance from the human standpoint. Yet the words of this girl carry conviction. They obviously express her faith. She speaks the truth. She has seen that Elisha is in truth a prophet of the Eternal. But once she has expressed this truth and thus borne testimony to her faith (and convinced Naaman), she vanishes from the story. There is no further reference to her; even her name is not recorded, and the rest of her human adventure is without importance. She has borne the Word of God, and this is the decisive event in her life both for herself and for others. We shall see, however, that later in the story God again uses very humble people, the servants of Naaman, who are also slaves, and pagans to boot.

Naaman angrily refuses to do what Elisha has had said to him through an intermediary (the supreme insult! the general has not even been "received"!). And now it is the slaves who decide the issue. It is not the prestige of Elisha, nor the power of the prophet, nor his word, which will convince Naaman. It is the banal words of his servants. Nor has the general any reason to believe his servants. He knows them well. He has plenty of evidence that they are not magi. And yet he is persuaded by the most simple of arguments which amounts to no more than this: "You can do this at all events. If it does no good, it will do no harm. It is not complicated. Why not try it?" This is the kind of thing we usually consider the very opposite of faith. But we have to admit that if in the last resort Naaman is swayed by this simple reasoning, it is because the argument is on his own level. This is an argument the natural man can listen to and accept. It is certainly not the saying of the prophet, and Christians must not take it as a model, but it is the kind of argument the ordinary man can address to the ordinary man, and we must be on guard against scorning it (even if we are not to overrate it either). God shows us that this is something he also uses.

In this' nexus of circumstances, of the free words of contingent men, through which a decision of God's will is effected, we thus see that God has plans for Naaman. Naaman has been chosen by God from among other lepers. Perhaps we might even surmise that if he is leprous, if there is this contradiction between his political power and his hidden distress, it is because God was waiting for him and planned through his mediation to penetrate the sphere of politics with the testimony to his love and also the presence of his truth. In a singular way, however, we shall see that in this story God's action is never clear, obvious, startling, unique, or incontestable, not even in the healing. For Naaman is still haunted by the idea of magic.

The waters of the Abana and the Pharpar are just as good a remedy as those of the Jordan. The Word of God is not in any way convincing or cogent in and of itself. God's commandment does not carry the evidence of truth and reason. On the contrary, it follows human paths each of which is both contestable and inadequate. God uses a host of concurrent agents to achieve his own end. There is the little girl who speaks with such deep conviction. There is the king of Syria who intervenes with the lofty disdain of power. There is Elisha who remains anonymous and absent, who does not even see Naaman, who encloses himself in the secret and mystery of the will of God. There are the servants who formulate the common-sense simplicity of the natural man. None of these alone can boast of having accomplished God's design. None can pretend that he is the central point in God's action, not even Elisha. For Elisha could have done nothing had not the little girl suggested that Naaman should come to him. And his word would have been in vain if the servants of Naaman had not provoked the general's obedience. Each, then, entered into the plan God had for the leper. Each had his own part. Each fulfilled his own vocation, whether wittingly (like Elisha) or unwittingly. But each intervened according to his own bent, at his own level, and with his own personal decision. Each was what he chose to be at the appropriate time. At no point do we find God forcing anyone by his own action. On the contrary, the whole story is designed to show that each intervenes freely and according to his own situation and with his own free remarks. The whole story is designed to display this independence of the individual in relation to God, who does not act in his subconscious and who does not condition him either directly or indirectly.

How can I state in this way that this is the point of the story? The case seems to me to be a very simple one. If the story wanted to show us God crushing the will of man and forcing man to do what God wants, then things would have been very simple. God would have sent Naaman directly to Elisha, and Naaman's obedience would have been pure and simple. We should thus have a schema repeated a thousand times in all the ancient and medieval legends, in which the relation between gods and men is precisely the relation of a crushing will with a man which makes a mere automaton of the will of the man himself. There is nothing in common with this here. Each acts according to his own intention. Only one man does not act. This is the prophet. The prophet knows what is God's intention for this man. He knows the gospel of God for the leper. He can disregard his own will, his own intention, his personal level of judgment. And he is the only one who does not act. All he does is intervene with the desperate king of Israel and have the leper sent to him. But he does not leave his own house to see and receive the general. He does not welcome him. He does not act. He simply has his servant tell him what is God's order regarding him. He does not preach the gospel to him, but with the promise he gives a command. All this ought to make us reconsider all the activist talk in the church, the supposed imperative that the church should go out to meet the world, the insistence that Christians should stop presenting to men the authoritative demand and commandment of God. . . . Now all the acts referred to are fragmentary and disconnected acts which have no significance alone. Similarly that of Elisha has no value of its own. It is God who weaves together the threads of these interventions, who makes of them an act of God, who brings to light their meaning and orientation. It is God who finally obtains what he hoped for by means of the liberty of each participant. But why in this way, through unimportant acts that are not connected to one another? The human link between them is obviously the person of Naaman, and if these acts are all petty, insignificant, and of no evident worth, it is because God respects the independence of Naaman just as he does that of each of the other characters in the story.

At every point the general has a decision to make. At every point this decision is not confronted by an irresistible constraint or by crushing evidence and certitude. He has to listen to what the little slave says. But why should he obey it? And even when the king of Israel sends him to Elisha, why should he not take umbrage and return to Syria to provoke the diplomatic incident? In addition, the word Elisha speaks to him is certainly not a compelling or totalitarian word. He can refuse to listen to it, and this is exactly why Elisha does not appear, why he treats him thus. This kind of anonymity which does not break through the television screen nor stun the middle-class citizen is God's great respect for the liberty of the one he loves. Naaman, too, has to decide for himself. He has also to do this in relation to what his slaves say to him. At every point in the story, then, each decides for himself what he has to do, and at every twist Naaman is confronted by a simple word which it is just as easy to set aside or ignore. This whole nexus finally serves to express the full gospel.

Yet the really puzzling thing in the story is that finally it all seems to be to no purpose. Certainly Naaman is cured. It is no little thing that a sick person is made well, especially a leper. But in the last resort there are still many other sick people. Again, Naaman undoubtedly perceives that this cure is God's act. He recognizes that this God is different from all the other gods, that there is no other god but the Lord. And this again is no little thing. We see that the miracle of which he was the object leads to his conversion. But what counts is probably not so much the facticity of the miracle as the signification Naaman perceives in it. He is surely struck by the difference between Elisha's action and that of all other magicians and sorcerers. He is struck by this mark of the power of this God, and perhaps even more so by the mercy of this God. All this is excellent. But apart from these two personal results for Naaman, what do we find? From the political standpoint first, the incident does not improve the situation between Israel and Syria nor stop the war which will very soon break out between them afresh. We see this war developing in Chapter 6, and historians agree that the same king of Israel figures in both stories. In other words Naaman, who continues to be a general, will probably lead the armies of Syria against Israel. His conversion does not change the relation between the powers. The church which is now present in both Syria and Israel does not stop politics being politics. And it is a great illusion to think that the church can prevent wars (although obviously this is not to say that it should endorse them). Furthermore, Naaman is still very superstitious. His conversion to the true God has not stripped away the beliefs of his background and civilization. He has not become a good theologian. In effect we see him asking for some of the soil of Israel, as much as can be carried by two mules, so that he can make a little bed of soil on which to build an altar to the Eternal. He is still convinced that God is a local God, that he is tied to a particular land. He is still convinced that if he carries away some of the soil of this land he will take with it a little of the presence of God. He is still convinced that God does not want to be worshiped except on the soil of this land which he willed to give to his people. He is still convinced that a sacrifice offered to God on other soil would not please him. To be sure these are all foolish notions, for us who are so spiritual that we have chased God off the earth and relocated him as far away as possible. But they are foolish notions which are not condemned by God himself.

The text does not tell us that Elisha corrects or condemns Naaman, nor that he gives him a lesson in theology. Naaman still entertains the ideas of his age, but he bends and subjugates them in the presence of the true God. It is to serve this true God that he acts in a way that seems ridiculous to us. It is in order to love exclusively, to make a rigorous demarcation, to affirm his break publicly, that, adopting the manners and ideas and customs of his day, he uses them to show that his God is not the same as that of others. Thus the very absurdity of his act is pleasing to God. "I am carrying the soil of Israel into Syria because the soil of Syria is not good." What an offense! There would have been no offense if he had rested content with a spiritual love of God. "I am carrying soil from elsewhere into Syria in order to bear concrete witness to the presence of the one true God who cannot be loved and served on this soil, the soil of Baal, Rimmon, and Ishtar." This is how faith transforms customs even though it leaves a man in his own culture. This is why we must not attempt the futile enterprise of demythologizing the Bible. One has only to read it to see where and how this demythologizing is done. Nevertheless, the ambivalence of Naaman's situation is not set aside. He takes a stand publicly. He makes a clean break by establishing his little plot for sacrifice. But from another angle he remains a politician, a councillor, a general. He is divided between his duty of state under an idolatrous prince and his faith in the Eternal. And the story continues to be surprising. He does not get the idea that as one who has been cured himself he must convert his king. He does not have the burning urge to witness. He shows none of the fire of the neophyte. Nor does he think of withdrawing, of becoming a hermit, of quitting his post. He is a politician and a soldier, and he remains so. "Every one should remain in the state in which he was called. Were you a slave when called? Never mind . . . " (1 Corinthians 7:20-21). Were you a general? Never mind. Yet he knows that the god he served up to this point, and the god his king continues to serve, is a false god. He knows that when he accompanies the king in ceremonies, he will seem to be worshiping this god. Publicly he will have to do what his position demands. He will have to bow down to Rimmon. He knows this is wrong. But he also knows he has no option but to do this wrong. He asks for forgiveness. This is another scandal.

He intends to sin and he asks for pardon in advance. We are faced here by an attitude which could hardly be more suspect and which opens the door to all kinds of compromises. This is "mental reservation." We act in one way publicly, but inwardly we do not believe it. We are inwardly free and this actually justifies our conformities to the present century. This is the attitude of Naaman, which he knows to be reprehensible. Nevertheless, this attitude has two positive aspects. Naaman expressly recognizes that Rimmon is an idol. He recognizes that this state service is disobedience to God, that his political action is open to condemnation. Are we so sure, when we serve idols, that we can see they are idols? Are we so sure we have the same clarity of vision in relation to the nation, the state, the independence of peoples, socialism, progress, the army, cultures, money, etc. When we choose to serve the powers that employ us, are we so sure we have the discernment of this general? "I can do no other; this is part of my service; but I know it is wrong." Are we so sure we have the honesty not to attempt to reconcile the two? This is the difference between Naaman's attitude and mental reservation. He does not seek inner reassurance. He does not separate the two spheres. He does not try to say that after all his secular service is willed by God even if it involves apparent worship of Rimmon—one cannot make omelettes without breaking eggs, it is impossible not to have dirty hands. Nor does he try to say that one might make a synthesis between God and Rimmon, that in apparently serving the latter one is really serving the former—we serve science or the state, but in reality we are serving God. He plainly admits the contradiction between the two. He admits that one cannot serve God and Mammon. But he sees no way out of the contradiction. He does not accept a compromise; he accuses himself. He does not try to pretend that he will henceforth be God's faithful servant by continuing to render service to the king, a service which will be disloyal because he no longer believes what he ought to believe as a Syrian general. From this point on he lives in inner strife and tension, since his position is in fact one that defies solution. It is that of every conscientious Christian who takes part in any way in the activity of society. And Naaman condemns himself. There is no other attitude he can take, no other outcome. His conduct may seem sometimes to be primitive (carrying the earth) or mediocre (not totally obeying God). Yet it is in very truth exemplary. He carries the earth and sets up an altar to God; this marks his break henceforth with his own earth, his country, and the gods of his fellow-citizens. He breaks with everything sacred in his society. He thus enters on the way of sanctity. Yet he also rejoins this society in a new relation. He continues to serve his king in repentance and in the conviction that although it is not finally good and righteous, nevertheless he ought to do it. This honesty in asking forgiveness in advance is precisely the sign of the authenticity of his conversion.

He speaks to Elisha and explains his situation. In some sense he seeks his counsel. He asks him to be his interpreter or mediator with the God he has now recognized to be the one true God. But in the main Elisha does not reply. He offers no ethical advice. He does not tell him he ought to leave his post and background and refuse to bow down before idols. Elisha does not plunge into casuistry, differentiating what would be legitimate for him from what would not. He has no solution to propose. He lets Naaman choose himself. He lets him make his own decision. He faces him up to his responsibility without saying what it is. Yet he does not let him go away empty. He grants him peace from God. He finally declares the gospel to him. Perhaps it should be noted that although Elisha did not receive the famous general when he came the first time from the king of Syria and also from the king of Israel, he did receive him the second time when this man came to make a confession of faith and to show him the conflict of faith. If Elisha did not receive him when it was a question of performing a miracle of healing for him (although he did perform it), he did receive him when the basic problem was at issue. And this, too, should be enlightening to us Christians who are so zealous for action and so scornful of what is only a matter of conversion and the inner life.

Elisha, then, gives him the blessing of peace. This means on the one hand that in spite of the tension between his faith and his public acts, peace is made with God. God has made peace and assures him of it. God sees beyond appearances. He knows the reality of the human heart. And since from now on the mighty general is poor in this conflict and penitence, he assures him of his peace. But again, when Elisha says: "Go in peace," this implies affirmation of the unity of Naaman's being. In spite of the tension, in spite of the rift between his faith and his conduct, in spite of the accusation his conscience brings against him, Naaman receives attestation that his being is not double, that he is one, that he exists in a unity that transcends the formal unity of the person. Naaman can now be what he is, not without questions and repentance, but whole and entire, a man who is no longer gnawed away by leprosy physically, a man who, resting in the peace of God, ceases to be gnawed away by the idolatry of the state which divides and corrupts the innermost depths of man.

Joram

2 Kings 6:24-7:17

24 Afterward Ben-hadad king of Syria mustered his entire army, and went up, and besieged Samaria. 25 And there was a great famine in Samaria, as they besieged it, until an ass's head was sold for eighty shekels of silver, and the fourth part of a kab of dove's dung for five shekels of silver. 26 Now as the king of Israel was passing by upon the wall, a woman cried out to him, saying, "Help, my lord, O king!" 27 And he said, "If the Lord will not help you, whence shall I help you? From the threshing floor, or from the wine press?" 28 And the king asked her, "What is your trouble?" She answered, "This woman said to me, 'Give your son, that we may eat him today, and we will eat my son tomorrow.' 29 So we boiled my son, and ate him. And on the next day I said to her, 'Give your son, that we may eat him'; but she has hidden her son." 30 When the king heard the words of the woman he rent his clothes—now he was passing by upon the wall—and the people looked, and, behold, he had sackcloth beneath upon his body—31 and he said, "May God do so to me, and more also, if the head of Elisha the son of Shaphat remains on his shoulders today."

32 Elisha was sitting in his house, and the elders were sitting with him. Now the king had dispatched a man from his presence; but before the messenger arrived Elisha said to the elders, "Do you see how this murderer has sent to take off my head? Look, when the messenger comes, shut the door, and hold the door fast against him. Is not the sound of his master's feet behind him?" 33 And while he was still speaking with them, the king came down to him and said, "This trouble is from the Lord! Why should I wait for the Lord any longer?"

1 Elisha said, "Hear the word of the Lord: thus says the Lord, Tomorrow about this time a measure of fine meal shall be sold for a

shekel, and two measures of barley for a shekel, at the gate of Samaria." 2 Then the captain on whose hand the king leaned[1] said to the man of God, "If the Lord himself should make windows in heaven, could this thing be?" But he said, "You shall see it with your own eyes, but you shall not eat of it."

3 Now there were four men who were lepers at the entrance to the gate; and they said one to another, "Why do we sit here till we die? 4 If we say, 'Let us enter the city,' the famine is in the city, and we shall die there; and if we sit here, we die also. So now come, let us go over to the camp of the Syrians; if they spare our lives we shall live, and if they kill us we shall but die." 5 So they arose at twilight to go to the camp of the Syrians; but when they came to the edge of the camp of the Syrians, behold, there was no one there. 6 For the Lord had made the army of the Syrians hear the sound of chariots, and of horses, the sound of a great army, so that they said one to another, "Behold, the king of Israel has hired against us the kings of the Hittites and the kings of Egypt to come upon us." 7 So they fled away in the twilight and forsook their tents, their horses, and their asses, leaving the camp as it was, and fled for their lives. 8 And when these lepers came to the edge of the camp, they went into a tent, and ate and drank, and they carried off silver and gold and clothing, and went and hid them; then they came back, and entered another tent, and carried off things from it, and went and hid them.

9 Then they said to one another, "We are not doing right. This day is a day of good news; if we are silent and wait until the morning light, punishment will overtake us; now therefore come, let us go and tell the king's household." 10 So they came and called to the gatekeepers of the city, and told them, "We came to the camp of the Syrians, and behold, there was no one to be seen or heard there, nothing but the horses tied, and the asses tied, and the tents as they were." 11 Then the gatekeepers called out, and it was told within the king's household. 12 And the king rose in the night, and said to his servants, "I will tell you what the Syrians have prepared against us. They know that we are hungry; therefore they have gone out of the camp to hide themselves in the open country, thinking, 'When they come out of the city, we shall take them alive and get into the city.' " 13 And one of his servants said, "Let some men take five of the remaining horses, seeing that those who are left here

[1] This was an officer who served as a third person in the chariot to support the king during journeys and battles.

will fare like the whole multitude of Israel that have already perished; let us send and see." 14 So they took two mounted men, and the king sent them after the army of the Syrians, saying, "Go and see." 15 So they went after them as far as the Jordan; and lo, all the way was littered with garments and equipment which the Syrians had thrown away in their haste. And the messengers returned, and told the king.

16 Then the people went out, and plundered the camp of the Syrians. So a measure of fine meal was sold for a shekel, and two measures of barley for a shekel, according to the word of the Lord. 17 Now the king had appointed the captain on whose hand he leaned to have charge of the gate; and the people trod upon him in the gate, so that he died, as the man of God had said when the king came down to him.

As we did not emphasize the miracle of healing or the problem of leprosy in the case of Naaman, so now we shall not dwell on what is usually the theme of commentaries, namely, the extraordinary action of God, the solution to the famine in Samaria, the sound of chariots in the Syrian camp. We shall not stress the fact that here is another instance of the omnipotence of God, who does what he wills, and of the love of God, who does not let his people perish. The lesson seems to me to be larger and more direct, and we shall make the characters in the story our primary consideration.

I

In this dreadful incident the king of Israel is the same as in the days of Naaman, King Joram, who is generally presented as a good king even though he was the son of Ahab and clung to the error of Jeroboam. He obviously maintained the traditional faith of Israel and we are told that he overturned the statues of Baal that his father had erected. When he was violently questioned by the woman, his reply was not derisive. The woman appealed to him for salvation. Her "save me" (*hochi-anna*) is highly ambiguous, for it might mean: Save my physical life by giving me food, but it might also mean: Save me before God. After all, our own S.O.S. has the same ambiguity. And in relation to this question of salvation the king draws back. If the reference is to material salvation from the famine, he cannot do anything, and even this is perhaps a manifestation of his orthodoxy. Some commentators think the mention of the threshing floor and the wine press in verse 27 is an allusion to the belief in Canaan (and it extended far beyond Canaan, for one finds it in almost all primitive peoples) that the king is the one who ensures fecundity, or good crops, and that his activity or (sexual) power is the guarantee of abundance for all. If so, then Joram's reply is: "I am not this kind of king. I am not like the king of Canaan, for the Eternal alone is the one who kills and makes alive." But his answer can also be given a spiritual sense: "It is not I who save but God. For myself I am nothing and I can do nothing." This is indeed a very correct and accurate and scrupulous theological position. No, Joram is not mocking the woman. Nevertheless, his answer is a momentous one, for he is also saying that he refuses to take the risk of faith. He leaves it to God because he refuses to be involved in the adventure himself. Now it is impossible for him not to be involved in it. For he is the king of Israel and this obviously means that he is the representative of God on earth. He is the Lord's anointed. He is the one who can take a divine decision. In declining to do so he is thus abdicating already as the true king of Israel. At this moment he loses his monarchy.[2] Let us take note that this concerns us all, for now in Jesus Christ we

---

2 As is shown by von Rad (*Old Testament Theology*, I [E. T.], p. 42) the monarchy does not have in the Northern Kingdom the same character as it does in Judah. It does not rest on a once-for-all choice made by Yahweh in David but on a choice which is renewed each time. Hence each king is endowed with a charisma granted by Yahweh. He thus represents in himself a force and a religious power.

are all invested with this power and we have no right to cloak ourselves in good theology in order to evade our responsibilities. Furthermore, in spite of his disclaimer, he is involved in this terrible adventure whether he wants to be or not. He is faced by the dreadful arrangement between the two women to eat their own children. The one refuses to give up her son and the other demands justice. For this is a matter of justice; the contract ought to be honored. Hence the king is involved again, for he is the guardian of right and justice. He must respect the conventions. He must be the judge in atrocious things. Yet he declines once more. He cannot pronounce justice in a matter like this. He cannot insist that the contract be upheld. Nor can he judge and condemn the woman who cries to him: "Save me." At this point we cannot but recall the other story about two infants and the judgment of Solomon. It would have needed the wisdom of Solomon, the true king of Israel, to pass judgment here. But Joram is not Solomon.

Let us take a further step. The king of the chosen people is faced by the most atrocious crime imaginable. A woman eats her child. She is not mad. It is a deliberate act. She does it by contract to save her own life. This is a sign which shows Joram how profound and total is the corruption of the chosen people. A member of this people is like that. And he—the king who represents the whole people, who is the synthesis in himself of the holy nation—he does nothing. He perhaps recognizes implicitly that in the presence of extreme suffering there are no more rules, there is no more morality, there is no more respect for anything. These women may be excused after all. Necessity knows no law. He does nothing but give way, lament, and repent. He rends his garments, and in this state he goes among the people and on the walls. He is the fallen king, the humbled man. He shows to all the people his weakness and his piety, for his piety is manifested in this repentance too. In face of the physical suffering and the monstrous crime he can only fall down before God and ask pardon for himself and his people. He undoubtedly has a proper sense of what penitence is. He has worn sackcloth to mortify himself before God—he, the king, in the name of the whole people. And he has kept this mortification secret, as Jesus will later say we should do. He has the conviction that he is king for repentance and chastisement. He bears the evil of all his people before God. He remains (or would like to remain) the guardian of spiritual things. And he does nothing.

We shall often have occasion to point out that in these stories the feverish activity of the believer is absurd. But we must now emphasize the very opposite. The king is the one who ought to act and intervene and direct. His true piety, his authentic repentance, is not enough. He needs wisdom, i.e., the science of government in accordance with God's will. And now suddenly this weak and pious king explodes into action. Elisha must be killed. Elisha is responsible for all this, for the military disaster and the moral disaster. For Elisha has always given assurance of God's faithfulness. He has promised God's help. But God has patently abandoned his people. Elisha must be put to death because it is he who carries God's Word, who constantly claims that God intervenes in our lives, and who finally represents God in Israel (the king forgets that he does too!). Behind Elisha, however, God is undoubtedly Joram's real target. The judgment is clear, man's judgment on God: "This evil comes from the Lord." It is God who is responsible. If he is Israel's God, how can he allow what is happening. The king could have endured without collapse the military defeat, the siege, and the physical misery of his people. But things have gone too far. In face of the horrible and abominable thing he has seen he can no longer believe that God is the living and loving God. In killing Elisha, the king is really getting at God.

Undoubtedly, the traditional conflict between king and prophet also breaks out again at this juncture. On the one side is the king, who is the normal and legitimate guardian of established and institutional religion, which is also willed by God (as we so often forget). On the other side the one who represents God is absolutely the wholly other, who cannot be reduced at all to any religious or theological form whatever, who is always absolutely new and surprising, who does not cease to come in the "today" of his presence, who disturbs our ritual, morality, and piety. On the one side is the guardian of what God has done and has been. His role is valuable, legitimate, and divinely willed in the absolute sense. For God is also the one who is constantly telling us in his Word to remember: Remember what I was for you yesterday. He is thus the guardian of true and correct tradition. On the other side is the son of thunder who interferes and overthrows, affirming that God is not the God of the past or of the dead, but the God of the present and the living. It is inevitable that conflict should break out. But we should always remember that both parties in the conflict are equally justified and are equally commissioned to fulfil a divine task. The king cannot tolerate disruption of the established order, and he is right, for he has been instituted precisely to protect and uphold this divinely willed order. He cannot accept the irrational adventure and revolutionary explosiveness of the Word spoken here and now.

Where he is wrong, however, is in playing off the God of yesterday against the God of today and in invoking God for the killing of the prophet, this prophet who in the king's eyes is involved in the scandal since he does not seem to be scandalized by the awful train of events which has brought on the king's spiritual crisis.

Finally, to complete the portrait of the king, we find a very characteristic trait. When the lepers come to announce the flight of the Syrians, the king sees in it a classic ruse or trap. They have pretended flight in order to draw us to the camp, and when we have sallied out they will come back and slay us. The king takes a rational and common-sense position. There was no reason for the Syrians to flee. Furthermore, the ruse of besiegers pretending to raise the siege was indeed a classic one. The king's judgment is thus the normal one any general or politician would reach in the circumstances. It is the attitude of reasonable doubt. Nor should we forget that it was a trait in the character of this king. What we see here we have seen already in the story of Naaman. When he received the letter from the king of Syria he interpreted it as a means of provoking war. One can hardly blame the king for taking this view. He was also the secular and military head of the people. He had to direct and govern it by the best methods, by strategy and reason. He had to use the human means of judgment at his disposal. What kind of king would that be who plunged blindly into every political and military snare? Any king would have thought as he did. The main difficulty for him was that he was not just any king.

He was the king of Israel, God's people. In this situation, however, he judged according to prudence and not according to faith. He did not listen to the Word that God had spoken to him. He did not see a Word of God in this whole incident. Now if it is common for man not to discern God's Word, this man who is part of the people of God has been invested at his election by the ability to hear and understand this Word. But now reasonable doubt and political prudence (which he must also exercise quite often) have snuffed out this ability to hear the Word of God when it is spoken to him. He is the man who has received the seed, who hears the Word, "but the cares of the world . . . choke the word, and it proves unfruitful" (Matthew 13:22). We are faced again by the serious problem of the politician. How can he avoid the cares of the

48

world? How can he fail to use prudence, competence, and reason? But how can this long-standing habit not choke the Word of God in its uncertainty, fragility, and unpredictability?

II

The second character in the story to whom we must now turn is the prophet. Now the story raises already the problem of what makes Elisha a prophet. It is certainly not the power of "sight" he displays in verse 32, the fact that he can see what goes on in the royal palace, that he knows what decision the king has made against him, that he is aware of the king's intention to assassinate him. Nor is it his power to foretell coming events (7:1), the fact that he declares that the people will be fed the next day. It is not even the miracle that ensues, the flight of the Syrians.

Now in the main facts of this kind are the marks of a prophet in our eyes. In reality, however, such facts are secondary. They accompany prophecy, but they do not constitute the prophet. They are not useless nor mythical. (Bultmannian spiritualizing, for which, if God is the Wholly Other, all these manifestations are just forms of expression with no real content, is certainly quite unacceptable, for why should not the Almighty be free to act in this way too?) But false prophets can also produce them, and so, too, can seers and magicians.

What constitutes the prophet is exact and rigorous proclamation of what God does, of God's decision, today. With objectivity, with, one might almost say, a certain indifference, a detachment as if it were no concern of his, the prophet says: "Look, God has decided this." But it is not just this unveiling (revelation) of the intention of God that makes a man a prophet. It is also the proclamation of an order: "Listen to the Word of God." There is something more important than trying to engage in trade, or to support oneself, or to watch on the walls, or to punish criminals: stop all that. Listen, now, to God's Word. The prophet offers a living Word for the present. He offers a Word relevant to the actual situation of men, a Word which will be a solution, but which is completely irrational and unexpected, and which implies for man a strange renouncing of his own methods and policies and normal inclinations. The prophet is in effect the man who brings a Word of God to bear on the actual, concrete situation of man, his political situation.

This is a Word which has no common denominator with our political intentions and appraisals. To come and say that among several political or economic systems this is a good one is not to speak a Word of God; to come and announce that it is necessary to belong to a particular party or union is not to speak a Word of God. To seek solutions to famine or political or colonial slavery is not to speak a Word of God. All this is Joram's attitude. Certainly the prophet shows that God is present in everyday life, in political dramas. But he does not bring any solution nor engage in any action. He shows but he does not demonstrate. He issues an order: Listen to the Word of God. You are now placed before it. Make your decision. At every point and turn, then, he adopts the starting-point of every attitude of faith. With the prophet there is no progress. There is no progress in the political situation (Naaman was cured but this changed nothing, for war broke out afterwards). There is also no progress in the spiritual situation. The prophet constantly brings us back to zero. The situation is always a completely new one. Our spiritual life is constantly brought back to the decision of faith, to that corner which our moral, theological, and ecclesiastical ruses seek in vain to avoid.

Yes or no, this time, will you listen to this Word of God?

But I already heard it yesterday.

We are now living today.

It's all the same.

But you are not the same, you have to decide today.

The prophet will not allow us to use faith as a point of departure for taking our journey through life or constructing our morality, ecclesiology, or politics. He addresses faith and demands the decision of faith now, for tomorrow will already be too late. He addresses faith, and only in the response of faith is the word that the prophet speaks a Word of God.

Again, Elisha makes no attempt at all to convince those who are not in faith. As we have seen, he does not demonstrate even to believers, and even less so when faced by unbelief. He pursues no apologetics at any level, whether objective or subjective. Yet in face of the proclamation of the Word, the first reaction Elisha can record is that of unbelief. The officer of the house shrugs his shoulders. What then? Will Elisha start again? Will he engage in discussion? Will he try to convince? Not at all. He simply announces to this man his situation before God: "You shall see it with your own eyes, but you shall not eat of it." The prophet sets aside this man who has refused. He tells him what concerns him, for his unbelief can be shamed only by his destiny. It sets him outside the truth of the Word but not outside the line of his life before God, and this is all that the prophet can say to him.

It is extraordinary to think that Elisha, who abounds in miracles, does not perform any miracle to confirm what he declares, whether to convince or to excite faith. But I think we must be bold and take the text in its entirety. What brought on the whole train of events was the woman's cry: "Save me." The king was then reduced to despair by the full horror of the situation. Then the prophet stepped in. There is a kind of parallelism with the story of Naaman. The general, too, was crying out: "Heal and save me." The king was again in despair and rent his clothes. In both cases he proclaimed that he could not respond to the cry: "Save me." In both cases the prophet stepped in. In answer to the scandalous question of the woman, to her ignoble and yet desperate situation, the prophet gave God's answer—a positive answer. To be sure, it was not a personal answer to the woman, whose act would no doubt come under judgment. But it was the collective answer of salvation given because one of these unfortunate people had pushed her despair to the extreme limit. Elisha, then, stood by his people. He, the prophet of God, did not remove himself to judge this people among whom such horrible things had been done. For we must not forget that in addition to the open crime of the woman many other heinous things afflicted the people, e.g., speculation and the crushing of the poor by the privileged, as is suggested by the note on the frightful prices for the least bit of nourishment. The prophet does not attack the people. He does not judge the woman or the speculators. He maintains solidarity with the people. He takes counsel with the elders. He comes to help what is still for him the people of God, the people to whom the Word of God must be spoken, no matter what the circumstances may be. And he also steps forth to announce to it the perseverance of the love of God even when everything seems to lead us to believe that the Eternal is no longer there. He steps forth to announce physical deliverance too.

But once again he does nothing. This is a strange thing to say, and we shall see again that in political problems the prophet remains inactive. He does not effect directly any intervention or miracle even to save himself. The king wants him put to death and sends a messenger to assassinate him. But the prophet does not use his power to save his life. This would have been easy enough for him when we think of all his other miracles. He does not employ any spiritual force. He refrains from asking God for protection. We are inevitably reminded of Jesus in Gethsemane: "Do you think that I cannot appeal to my Father, and he will at once send me more than twelve legions of angels?" (Matthew 26:53). But he did not appeal, and neither did Elisha. Elisha uses purely human means. He closes the doors. He protects himself like anyone else. In this very real danger he does not think he should use his power on his own behalf. God's power has not been given to him for his own advantage. He takes refuge behind a closed door, and for the moment this flimsy barrier must serve as his only security. For good or ill, therefore, Elisha remains among the men of this Israel of God now that they are in the very depths of misfortune.

This does not mean, however, that he is all sweetness, hope, and charity. He pronounces judgments, judgments against the king and against the officer of the guard. The king who is still Israel incarnate: Joram the son of the assassin, for Joram is indeed the son of Ahab, murderer of the prophets of Yahweh, and also murderer of Naboth (the miserable little story of Naboth continually comes up again); Joram himself an assassin, for it is his intention to continue his father's work and to slay the prophet—the king is judged; everything converges now. We have seen above that he unwittingly renounces his role, his office as Israel's king (v. 30). Now with his decision to have Elisha put to death he brings down on himself the express condemnation of the Word of God. This twofold development will take place when Elisha will go to anoint Jehu and to have the king dethroned.

But there is another judgment too. It is on the officer, who finds himself excluded from the promise made to the people. The prophet does not condemn him directly; he simply answers his unbelief. In effect he is condemned to death. The prophet's condemnations certainly pose the problem of final judgment, of the ultimate salvation of men, of the range of these judgments. Do the words pronounced against the officer and the king, as Words of

God, carry with them the eternal damnation of these men? Is God no longer God-with-them? Are these condemnations a final judgment on them? They have not had faith; they are judged already (John 3:18). Or may it be that what we have here are only actual, temporal, and temporary signs of this final judgment, which should serve as warnings as to the seriousness of the Word of God, but which do not necessarily imperil the salvation of these two men for whom Jesus also dies? My own conviction is that in all this we simply have a rejection in time, a condemnation for the moment, not eternal damnation.

They are thus condemned but not damned. They are put outside God's work but not his love. Historians tell us there was no concept of eternal life or of resurrection in ancient Israel. Hence there was no thought of eternal retribution in good or evil. Everything took place on earth. God's judgments had validity only for this world. Only with the development which led to the concept of eternal life did another dimension come to be given to the judgment of God. All this may be true, but it is hardly adequate, for we are now confronted by the unity of this Scripture which is recognized in its entirety by faith to be the one Word of God, unique, total, and complete. In this one Word of God we do in fact find two types of eternal decisions regarding man. Some decisions concern his concrete life on earth. Here, too, there may be rejection, condemnation, and chastisement. Each brings down this decision upon himself, and this decision of God can be of infinite seriousness and severity. For after all there is here a twofold condemnation to death. The one may be executed immediately or a dozen years later, it makes no odds. Then we have God's judgment on the inner core of the problem, on the final relation between this man and God. It is here that Jesus Christ is offered up as an expiatory victim, as a ransom from bondage to death, as God taking man's place beneath the justice of God. This is also true for Joram and the officer.

But in making this distinction are we returning to ancient ideas? Is the historical rejection in time an expiation for our faults on earth? Is there an earthly punishment even as we await salvation in heaven? To say this is in effect to nullify the work of Jesus Christ. If we are smitten on earth to expiate our faults, then temporal judgment is the same as eternal judgment. But this is not what we learn from the Bible. Are we not arguing that there is a correlation between happiness and obedience to God (or faith), between unhappiness and revolt against God, according to the ancient theory debated in the Book of Job? But again this does not seem to me at all to be the biblical teaching. Furthermore, in these conditions, to what would God's historical judgment correspond in the concrete life of man? It seems to me that the position is always very clear: God speaks. To this actual, living, present Word of God addressed to a man there must be the reply of an actual, present decision of faith. Now when God speaks to a man, it is never for his personal satisfaction, for the sake of his soul or his happiness. The announcement God makes to him is always connected with an order God gives him, a service he expects of him, a mission he lays upon him. And the reply of faith that God expects is that the man will accomplish this mission and service, that he will enter into God's design. But when the man refuses to do this, when he does not accept the word as a Word of God, when he takes refuge behind doubt, or eternity, or human wisdom, when this man asks God to wait, then God rejects him, but he does not send him to hell. He discards him as an instrument he cannot use. God has a work to do. He calls a man. This man refuses or does not hear. So God dismisses him and calls another. The first man called is not outside God's love nor outside salvation in Christ. But he is out of work. He has been dropped from the great adventure, the great history, of salvation. He no longer has a place in God's plan. God depended on him to say yes or no. He has chosen not to be involved. God accepts his decision. King Joram is no longer the real king of Israel. He is of no use even though he continues to engage in politics and to make wars, even though he is very active and makes alliances. All this is irrelevant. It is outside God's plan. His enterprises may be discounted by historians. They are just a blank in the work of God. This is the meaning of temporal rejection, just as temporal election is always election for service. To be sure, this temporal rejection is for the spectator a sign and a warning. It reminds him of the extreme seriousness of the Word which is spoken to us. The king's officer who is crushed to death should not only be a warning in this world. He should also send us back to the infinite grace of God in Christ which changes every condemnation into pardon, or rather which sets every condemnation within the infinite love of God, who punishes to three generations but who pardons to a thousand generations.

Perhaps another question should be raised. Why do we find two different attitudes in the prophet? Why does he not condemn the faults of the people and those of the women who have committed a crime? Conversely, why does condemnation fall on the king and his officer? The answer seems to be quite simple and in conformity with the total teaching of Scripture. In the former case we have moral faults. These are also very important, and sometimes the prophets deal specifically with them. It is certainly no light thing to kill an infant. Indeed, the very reason why there is no reference to the judgment of God on those who commit such crimes, to the judgment of God which falls on his Son, is that nothing can expiate this kind of offense. Here we cannot but be in the presence of this judgment. It cannot be just a matter of refusing service or of not obeying the actual order of God. In the case of the king and the officer, however, the problem is very different. An express Word of God is addressed to them. Before this

56

Word they have to decide. The Word is spoken to them in the first instance because they are responsible at this point. They are guides and authorities for the people. They have to make a decision of faith, a decision for service, to follow and to obey this Word which is spoken to them personally. And the one says: "Why should I wait for the Lord any longer," while the other shrugs his shoulders: "If the Lord himself should make windows in heaven, could this thing be?" This doubt, this refusal of service, provokes the judgment of temporal rejection. The people in its misery has obeyed the law of necessity and done wrong, but God has profound pity on the man who is brought down thus. But the man who receives God's Word is restored to liberty. The king and the officer to whom the Word is addressed in the first instance have become free to decide, and they are thus in very truth responsible for their refusal to obey. They are without any excuse. They have no recourse apart from the final recourse in Christ.

III

We now come to the central problem which will constantly confront us in these pages. This is the problem of the relation between God's decision and man's. We should first stop to consider God's own attitude. For if Scripture says little about God's being or essence, it is constantly revealing his action and presence. Without doubt the first thing to strike us here is the pure freedom of God's decision. We can find no reason at all for his attitude. Why, for example, does he allow the invasion of Israel? Why is Samaria reduced for the second time to this extremity? Why this distress? Israel is no worse than other peoples. It is no worse at this moment in its history than at other moments. There is no reason, motive, cause, or condition for God's free will. God is God. He speaks, and things are. We have not to think that behind there might be something different. This unhappy people is again led into even greater evil by the trial itself. Under the suffering of the siege it does not prove to be heroic or virtuous. On the contrary, crime and oppression increase. One might say that God leads his people into an excess of iniquity. Conversely, there is no reason why the trial should cease. There is no comprehensible motive for God's arresting of the situation and raising of the siege. We wish we could say: "He will not let you be tempted beyond your strength" (1 Corinthians 10:13). But one has the impression this unhappy people has in fact been tempted beyond this point. No, God is not even conditioned by this limitation. He chooses the moment of deliverance, too, in absolute freedom. Neither prayer nor the king's repentance forces his hand. One day the Word of God will break over man and declare: "Lo, the trial is over." This moment is God's secret. We are faced here by the same freedom as that which Jesus preserved when he spoke of the end of the ages and said that even the Son has no knowledge on this subject. No preconceived, discernible, or revealed plan exists. There is no premonitory sign that we can calculate. There is no passage of time corresponding to historical periods. No doing of works, no achievements of missions or churches, no propagation of the gospel, no excess of human sufferings, can cause us to say: "Lo, to-morrow. . . ." The Word which will say this will come upon us like the eagle when no one expects it, when no one expects it any more. And I think this strict freedom of God explains all those New Testament texts which historians persist in regarding as written as a result of the mistaken ideas of the first Christians who expected the immediate return of the Lord and were bitterly surprised when it was delayed.

Perhaps the words used may be explained by some such misunderstanding, but the explanation as such is a trite one. For the words express the truth of the freedom of

God, who is counselled and controlled by nobody. This is the God, then, who lets the suffering of man go on, who is deaf to his cry, who does not prevent the persecution, who for some time grants neither deliverance nor answer to prayer, so that one can understand the accusation of man against him, the accusation of the king: "This trouble is from the Lord!" Yes, one must accept it. If God is the author of all things. . . . Yet it should be noted that the king makes the accusation only after hearing of the crime of the two women. The king has withstood without flinching the siege, the defeat, the famine. But in face of this moral evil, this scandal, he has reached his limit. As the king of Israel he can no longer bear the burden of such abominations. Not I, but God is now responsible for these atrocities. And it is true that God's absolute freedom in these matters leads us to this conclusion. Now when he is faced by this accusation, which is repeated a hundredfold by man against God, and which finds an echo in the Bible, God never answers. God does not explain his conduct and decision to man when the latter demands an account, just as God does not justify himself before man. This is the same problem as that of Job. Job, too, accuses God of being the author of evil. And when at last, after a long debate and the prolonged cry of suffering man, God speaks, he does not explain or reply to Job.

There is no theology of expiation, of testing, or of the presence of Satan. All the hypotheses suggested and discarded by Job and his friends are discourses to which no answer is given. God does not choose to set his stamp on any of them. He reveals only one thing to Job, namely, that he is the free God, the unrestricted God, the God who gives an account to no one. But he is also the God who speaks *to* this man and who is thus *with* this man. This is enough to demolish all objections, accusations, theogonies, revolts and dramas. "I have uttered what I did not understand" (Job 42:3). This is all that man can ultimately say when confronted by the revealed freedom of God. Here too, then, God neither explains nor justifies himself when accused by the king. But the prophetic word is uttered at once; in face of the accusation God replies by asking for faith. "Tomorrow," says the prophet, tomorrow there will be full liberation, everything will be resolved and accomplished. Today you have to receive this promise and believe. You have to stop questioning and believe and wait for tomorrow. Things do not happen at once. There is no explosion of miraculous deliverance. All that is given is just a man's word: Tomorrow. And this is finally the real test to which God is leading man. In his suffering and rebellion today, will he be capable of discerning the presence of God himself in this word? Will he have the patience to wait (he who after many months is waiting for the end of the siege, we who after many centuries wait for the Lord's return)? Will he have the patience to wait for tomorrow? The prophet gives no direct answer to the accusation of the king. He does not engage in theological discussion. He announces that absolutely free grace will reply to faith. He restricts himself to this announcement. In other words, the problem is not a metaphysical problem. The existence of evil, its cause, God's attitude to it, the relation of God's omnipotence to it—these are all matters for an irrelevant metaphysical dissertation. To have knowledge of such things changes nothing whatsoever in our life and sufferings. The doctrine of evil and its origin may satisfy our curiosity but it is unimportant. God is not an encyclopedia whose task is to satisfy our curiosity. The true question is that of man's attitude in the situation of suffering and the grip of evil. The king revolts; it is God's fault. He is in despair; what more is there to hope for? The prophet simply calls for faith. No wave of a magical wand can change the evil metaphysically into good, or offer an explanation of it, or modify the objective situation of man. An appeal is simply made to the changing of man in the presence of God's promise. You are in despair in a hopeless situation. But God's Word is addressed to you. Tomorrow you will receive (exactly as in the case of the manna in the wilderness, you have to believe each day that you will receive your ration tomorrow). Today, believe. To God's total freedom, which man can only accept, there should be a response of faith even though no sign is given him today, no sign, in our case, apart from Jesus Christ.

This freedom of God finds expression also in the choice of the means he employs. Samaria will be saved, but to accomplish this God neither uses nor relies on the courage of the soldiers, the skill of the generals, the politics of the king, or the return of all the people to virtue and morality. God will save Samaria by a miracle. He will do it by the most ridiculous, empty, and illusory miracle, by a noise, a wind, an echo, by an illusion which makes a victorious army flee. This is an illustration of the fact that God chooses "things that are not, to bring to nothing things that are" (1 Corinthians 1:28). But it also shows how much noise and how little weight or worth or significance there is in what man does. I think that we who take our politics and bombs and elections so seriously should take this seriously too. Here we have a victorious army, a devastating war, imperial politics, and then an echo; there is nothing left. God in heaven does indeed laugh to scorn the furious raging of the people (Psalm 2:1ff.). He laughs at our political passions and our military and revolutionary storms. All this, serious enterprises included, has precisely the dimension and the value of a noise. In truth the dramas of the nations belong to this level, so that no one can finally glory in what results. Neither the king of Israel nor his army can indeed be triumphant. We need to be convinced in all our political actions (and they are far from being futile) that we too have no reason to be triumphant.

But God is not content with a miracle in which men have no part at all. He always associates man with himself in his acts and in the execution of his work, for his work is done on man's behalf.

His work is not abstract. It makes sense only if man grasps and utilizes it. The miracle is not for its own sake. The fact that the Syrians flee means nothing in isolation. Israel has to have a part in what God does. It has to profit by the miracle. The mere fact that the Syrians flee solves nothing for Israel if the latter does not show the attitude of faith which consists in believing that the miracle has taken place. (Believe that you have received already, says Jesus Christ.) The miracle alone is not a miracle. It is a miracle when man accepts and adopts it as such. Here again we see God's freedom in the choice of means. God chooses some men among others. He associates men secondarily with himself in the doing of his work. But what men? Not the most qualified, the most informed, the most worthy, the most alert. We see God choose lepers to discover the miracle just as it is women coming to the tomb with their own material concerns who discover the great miracle. The lepers are rejects. They are unclean. They are specially marked by traces of sickness and the sign of sin. They have been rightly thrust out of the camp and they have no further part in religious life. But it is to these lepers that God gives a place and a task in his miracle. Then at the other end of the story, to execute his judgment, God chooses the crowd, man in his most animal state, at his most unreflecting and irrational. It is man who does what God expects, but certainly not the kind of man that man himself would have chosen for so lofty a function.

Nevertheless we see that for all his freedom God respects the word of the man who adopts and declares it. The prophet's word is indisputably fulfilled by God. There is no point in pressing this or in raising the insoluble problem whether God caused the prophet to say what he did because he willed that this be done or whether God listened to the word of his prophet and, because he loved him, accomplished what he had said. This is a false dilemma, for both aspects are equally and simultaneously correct. We know indeed that God can sometimes expressly command his prophet to intimate something and then God does not do it, as in the case of Jonah. God treats the king's saying with the same freedom. The king said: "May God do so to me, and more also, if the head of Elisha . . . remains on his shoulders today." The head of Elisha did not fall. But God is not invoked in vain. The king himself will be rejected and then put to death. There is need to reflect on this decision and condemnation. God shows hereby that he governs the king and the monarchy. He gives a reminder that he is still the true king of his people, that it is he (and not this feeble king) who commands in Israel, delivers Israel, and serves as its commander-in-chief, that it is he also (and not this king that abdicates his responsibility) who himself bears all the suffering of this people, who takes it to himself and suffers it, that finally it is on him (and not on this blind king) that there falls all the evil committed among his people. This people remains the people of God, and the king of this people, even though rejected, remains a symbol of the true king of this people. What happens with the rejection of the king is what will happen to the true king of the people of God. The dreadful evil, the crime committed, God himself takes it upon himself and will manifest it in his Son Jesus Christ.

IV

Thus everything rests on God's freedom, and yet the truly astonishing feature in these stories is that everything rests also on human decisions. These are real decisions and not just acts or good works done in obedience to God and in response to his known will, his law, his clear commandment. The prophet gives no order to act. He does not head an operation. He declares what will happen but does not ask specific people to step in. Man himself will choose his own acts for human motives at the level of reason or intuition. The whole story makes it clear that man is not "mechanized" or "inspired" by God. Each man chooses his own way for his own reasons.

We first find the intervention of the lepers. They are outside the town as the law demands (Leviticus 13:46). They live on alms, and in this time of famine gifts are few and far between. They have been shown no special favor by God, for, unlike Naaman, they have not been cured. Once again God seems to be leaving the members of his people aside. They are put in a situation of what one might almost call fate, and we find them reasoning in a very realistic and natural way. If we go into the city we shall certainly die (of hunger or stoning). But if we stay here we shall die just as certainly, for there is no one to feed us. If we go to the Syrians it is possible they might kill us, as lepers and Jews. But it is also possible they might not kill us, and we should then have something to eat. Their choice is dictated by the realistic and irrefutable logic of necessity. They thus act at a strictly human level. The rest of their conduct is also characterized by the same humanity in this restricted sense. When they find the camp empty they help themselves first. They plunder and pillage. They hide their own little piles of loot. They think of themselves first, and it is not for us to blame them, or to moralize; we may simply emphasize that they were not virtuous Israelites anxious to discover and to understand the will of God. No, they acted exactly like any other man without God whose motto is: "Self first; let us profit by the occasion." Nor is their second impulse better than the first. Having satisfied their own needs they then tackle the moral problems and take "religious" stock of the situation. "We are not doing right" (it is a little late to see this), and "if we are silent . . . punishment will overtake us," surely the very lowest "religious" level: a moral vision of the situation before God; repentance out of fear; the idea of a God who punishes according to the balance of good and bad. Here again we have the reaction of the natural man and natural religion. The conduct of these lepers continues to be worthy of note. With the prudence which is customary in such matters, they do not tell their wonderful news to the people and those most concerned. They make their report to the authorities by the chain of command, i.e., from the gatekeepers to the king (for they themselves have no right of entry into the city and they accept their position). Nevertheless, these men who act at a strictly human level, who give no evidence of any spiritual or moral quality, who simply make an objective report on the situation they themselves have seen, these men do exactly what God expected. It is they who confirm the fulfilment of the prophecy. But did they actually know this prophecy of the day before? Almost certainly not. They were outside the city. They have a part in the miracle and yet they do not know that it is a miracle or that God announced it. They see an event and they draw the usual human conclusions. Nevertheless, they are witnesses of the fulfilment; they come to tell the good news to the people of Israel.

We are not forcing the text. The word employed is "good news," normally used for news which comes from God, which announces a divine act. In this sense it is not entirely fanciful to claim that they were, as Vischer says, the four evangelists carrying the good news of deliverance and salvation.

It is in the same sense that the women at the empty tomb were the evangelists of the resurrection. But we notice that this was all unintentional. Or rather, their own clear intention, their conscious decision, their express motivation, had a dimension and signification they could not realize. They could not know the underlying background of their own word and their own will. We see how their own will was inwardly caught up in the intention of God, who did not constrain them in any way. Their free decision was given a place in the secret and vaster plan of God. Others could have filled their role. But it was they who filled it. And they did so without any intention whatever of doing God's will in this sense.

Along exactly the same lines we next find the free and prudent decision of the king (v. 13). He too, as we have seen, follows purely human motives. He weighs things politically. The decision he reaches (to send five of the thinnest horses with two chariots) is dictated by distrust, prudence, and a concern to risk as little as possible. It is certainly very far from being the decision of faith, of total risk, which God asks us to make. It is the very opposite of the all or nothing which God risked but which we dare not accept.

The king had no faith at all in the Word of God declared by Elisha. Nor did he believe the leper evangelists or their eyewitness. He reacted like a suspicious king, and after free political calculation he took a chance (perhaps this is true after all?) but obviously in such a way that if nothing was gained nothing would be lost, i.e., as little was risked as possible. But again this decision of mistrust (or little faith), of man's prudence and common-sense, of scepticism, finds a place precisely in God's design. One might almost say that the king had to make the decision or choice to verify exactly the fulfilment of the prophecy. But for him, too, there was no connection between the prophet and what he had been told; no connection whatever. In his political reckoning, however, he played spontaneously the role which was indispensable if the intention of God for the people was to be accomplished and the prophecy was to be genuinely fulfilled, not just in itself, but for the people which God had resolved to save.

Finally we come across a third remarkable conjunction in the action of the crowd. Once the good news is verified it is spread abroad among the people. Once it is known by the people, the mob is unleashed. There is obviously no holding back these starving wretches who have simply been awaiting death in some way, whether by famine if the siege continues or by the sword if there is a victorious assault. Suddenly the twofold danger has been lifted. They do not stop to talk about it, except perhaps to ask initially how it has happened and to recognize briefly how it relates to Elisha's prophecy—as we know from the text—which is a result of this kind of reflection. No, there is an instantaneous rush for food. This is liberation. The crowd is unleashed. And again it is every man for himself. The main aim is to get there first so as to get the greatest possible amount of food at once, as though there was not enough for everyone. The crowd obeys its own violence, its own elemental impulse. It is the equivalent of panic, but in a forward rush. And in a crowd unleashed in this way, there are inevitably casualties.

The officer of the king who is at the gate is one of those trampled by the mob. The mob does not crush him intentionally. Yet on this bestial level, through a crowd which is only following its own instincts, God's judgment is executed. The mob is not an instrument of God. It is not constrained to act by a divine push but by its hunger and the news of food. It simply acts according to the nature of a panic-stricken mob, and that is all. It has no desire to do anything relating to the Word of God. Yet, obeying its own violent impulse, it does just what God expects. In one way or another the officer was condemned, and man decided in what way, even though he did not realize he was carrying out the divine sentence.

Now we must beware of generalization. We certainly cannot say that every time a man acts without thinking, that every time he follows his instinct, he executes a divine judgment. Nevertheless, one has to consider that this is also possible; it cannot be ruled out.

In this full and complex story, then, we find conjoined a

miracle and the most banal of human reflection. We find God's intention fulfilled through a series of free human choices, some strong and some very feeble. We find human decisions intermeshed without any need of divine intervention (for perhaps even the Syrian flight was a phenomenon of mob panic such as can be spontaneously produced). We also find some human decisions that are integrated into God's decision, while others are not. We learn first that God's action is certainly not governed or provoked by man. Yet God takes account of man's distress and his repentance, of his appeals and his revolts. The moment and means of God's intervention are undoubtedly unknown to us and cannot be foreseen or grasped. At no point is God determined by anyone save himself. What we see already in the story, however, is that God intervenes because he remains the God of this people. He intervenes because the one who incarnates the people, who should normally represent God to the chosen people, the king, ceases to fulfil this role and is no longer the true king. At this moment God takes upon himself the misery of this people, its shame, and the evil that it commits. One might almost say that what "determines" God's action in a given circumstance is that God takes upon himself the evil and the misery of man. Referring this to Jesus Christ, we may say that what determines the action and decision of God here and now is that he has taken upon himself all the misery of man and all the revolt of man in his Son Jesus Christ: all the misery and all the evil, including that of the particular situation which we are now living out in our own lives. God intervenes in this situation precisely for this reason. This is just another way of saying that God loves every man at every moment in every specific situation as he loved his Son Jesus Christ: not more (for Jesus Christ was delivered up to temptation, to testing, to fatigue, to hunger, to suffering and to death), but not less.

Reciprocally, man's action is not determined by God

any more than that of Jesus Christ was. We always have voluntary action. Wittingly or unwittingly man obeys his calculations, his needs, his passions, and his fears. God grants man freedom to do other than God expects, i.e., to do evil. He grants him the freedom to choose. All the same, everything man does is within the global plan of God. In all the complexity of human choices and interventions, some of them finally participate in this plan, fulfilling and accomplishing it. It is not that there is a preformed plan of God into which the actions of man fit as in a jigsaw puzzle. But in harmony with the perfect will of God, which is both holy and merciful, some human actions are taken by God and used by him to do his work. It is not that there is a work of God in which the actions of man are inserted (and even less mechanically produced). There are works of man—although not all man's works—which God utilizes for his own work. We do not have a mixture or fusion of God's will and man's. Everything that is perfect, everything that is of eternal validity, is God's will. But none of it is done by anyone but man. Not that man can do anything perfect or holy in and of himself. But God takes from man's work that which he will make perfect and eternal. Thus one cannot say that on the one side there is in the absolute sense a history of mankind and then independently a history of God or work of God. It is equally wrong, however, to say something that is often advanced today, namely, that the history of mankind is finally the history of God himself with all the sorry deductions drawn from the fact that Jesus is Lord of history, etc. In the vast medley of private and public actions and political and economic decisions, in the enormous and incomprehensible complexity of the history of men, some decisions and works finally accomplish the intention of God, or are at least chosen and adopted by him. Certainly it is man who accomplishes all the history, who does God's will in this history. It is man alone. But in this medley, this swarm, this chaos, this proliferating incoherence of man, there is a choice that is God's choice. If the situation is always fashioned by man and God is ready to put himself in it (because he is with man); if God subjects himself to the incoherences and absurdities of man (which he has done in the delivering up of Jesus Christ to men); if the jumble of human decisions constitutes a "history" that historians can write, this does not mean either that all man's actions are retained by God, nor that the situation is right, nor that there is a shade of progress, nor that the history corresponds to what God himself has resolved to do.

It is never possible to see what act of man does in fact fulfil the will of God. This we shall see only in the final recapitulation of all things in Christ when the greater part of the human agitation we call history will sink into nothingness. But what we need to know now is that it is man and he alone, and for his own motives, who manifests willy nilly the hand which gives and takes away, which slays and makes alive.

But again we must add three remarks. The first is that this fulfilment by man is set in the stream of global, political, and economic history even when we seem to have only private decisions (like that of the lepers).

The second is that it is all set within the people of God and in relation to it. To be sure, we are speaking of the history of men, but of a history which is coordinated with the history of Israel and the church. Certainly it is not the latter history that gives meaning to the history of man. Nevertheless, the history of man is indissolubly bound up with this history, and it is in this relation that God's decision plays its part.

Thirdly, this doing of God's will by man in his daily choices obviously does not discharge him from willing obedience as well. No reassurance can be found in the evasion that there are in the totality of my daily actions

70

some which are pleasing to God, which are chosen by him, even though I do not know which these are and even though my most commonplace acts may also serve the divine plan, so that I have no need to try to find out what is God's will, nor to attempt to do good, nor to enter voluntarily into his design. This type of argument is mere self-justification and hypocrisy. Once the Word of God has been addressed to me (and this applies equally to the king and to the officer), it must be my foundation on which I try to find out what can fulfil it and accomplish it among my acts and decisions.

I have to realize that what will finally be retained by God is not necessarily what I have done with the greatest piety, morality, faith, or searching out of the will of God. I have to realize that the acts I think indifferent might be the very ones that God retains, although he does not have to retain these either. I have to remember Matthew 25: I am still a rebel, a hypocrite, a liar, a blasphemer of God if I use all this to shuffle off the responsibility of doing expressly what God expects of me, to deny the commandment, the order, the explicitly stated will of God. We shall come back again and again to the same crooked human thinking: If God can use anything, I can do anything. This is to treat God with contempt: If I am in any case an unprofitable servant, I do not have to bother about what is profitable as God clearly reveals it in his law. This is the self-justification of a capitalist-type speculator. We have always to remember that it is after and not before I have done all that is commanded (in both faith and order) that I must pass upon myself the judgment of being an unprofitable servant.

The situation of the man to whom the Word of God has not been expressly declared, but whose decisions are also taken up by God, is completely different from that of the man who has received this knowledge, for the latter has no right to avoid an express attempt to fulfil the commandment, without which he falls under judgment like the king and the officer.

All the acts which I have done expressly to serve thee, and also all the acts which I believe to be neutral and purely human, and also all the acts which I know to be disobedience and sin, I put in thy hands, O God, my Lord and Savior; take them now that they are finished; prove them thyself to see which enter into thy work and which deserve only judgment and death; use, cut, trim, reset, readjust, now that it is no longer I who can decide or know, now that what is done is done, what I have written I have written. It is thou that canst make a line true by taking it up into thy truth. It is thou that canst make an action right by using it to accomplish thy design, which is mysterious as I write now but bright in the eternity which thou hast revealed to me in thy Son. Amen.

Hazael

2 Kings 8:7-15; 13:14-25

7 Now Elisha came to Damascus. Ben-hadad the king of Syria was sick; and when it was told him, "The man of God has come here," 8 the king said to Hazael, "Take a present with you and go to meet the man of God, and inquire of the Lord through him, saying, 'Shall I recover from this sickness?'" 9 So Hazael went to meet him, and took a present with him, all kinds of goods of Damascus, forty camel loads. When he came and stood before him, he said, "Your son Ben-hadad king of Syria has sent me to you, saying, 'Shall I recover from this sickness?'" 10 And Elisha said to him, "Go, say to him, 'You shall certainly recover'; but the Lord has shown me that he shall certainly die." 11 And he fixed his gaze and stared at him, until he was ashamed. And the man of God wept. 12 And Hazael said, "Why does my lord weep?" He answered, "Because I know the evil that you will do to the people of Israel; you will set on fire their fortresses, and you will slay their young men with the sword, and dash in pieces their little ones, and rip up their women with child." 13 And Hazael said, "What is your servant, who is but a dog, that he should do this great thing?" Elisha answered, "The Lord has shown me that you are to be king over Syria." 14 Then he departed from Elisha, and came to his master, who said to him, "What did Elisha say to you?" And he answered, "He told me that you would certainly recover." 15 But on the morrow he took the coverlet and dipped it in water and spread it over his face, till he died. And Hazael became king in his stead.

14 Now when Elisha had fallen sick with the illness of which he was to die, Joash king of Israel went down to him, and wept before him, crying, "My father, my father! The chariots of Israel and its horsemen!" 15 And Elisha said to him, "Take a bow and arrows";

so he took a bow and arrows. 16 Then he said to the king of Israel, "Draw the bow"; and he drew it. And Elisha laid his hands upon the king's hands. 17 And he said, "Open the window eastward"; and he opened it. Then Elisha said, "Shoot"; and he shot. And he said, "The Lord's arrow of victory over Syria! For you shall fight the Syrians in Aphek until you have made an end of them." 18 And he said, "Take the arrows"; and he took them. And he said to the king of Israel, "Strike the ground with them"; and he struck three times, and stopped. 19 Then the man of God was angry with him, and said, "You should have struck five or six times; then you would have struck down Syria until you had made an end of it, but now you will strike down Syria only three times."

20 So Elisha died, and they buried him. . . .

22 Now Hazael king of Syria oppressed Israel all the days of Jehoahaz. 23 But the Lord was gracious to them and had compassion on them, and he turned toward them, because of his covenant with Abraham, Isaac, and Jacob, and would not destroy them; nor has he cast them from his presence until now.

24 When Hazael king of Syria died, Ben-hadad his son became king in his stead. 25 Then Jehoash the son of Jehoahaz took again from Ben-hadad the son of Hazael the cities which he had taken from Jehoahaz his father in war. Three times Joash defeated him and recovered the cities of Israel.

We now come up against a new aspect of the same relation. We see historical events unroll according to the word of the prophet. To be specific, Elisha provokes a *coup d'état* in Syria, brings about a dynastic change, and then provokes a similar *coup d'état* in Israel and Judah. The prophet himself intervenes directly to make Hazael king of Syria and Jehu king of the two kingdoms.

But we are faced at once by a preliminary problem. What Elisha does has not been directly or expressly commanded by God. He does what in fact Elijah had been ordered to do. This was in the days of Ahab. After the victory over the prophets of Baal, the demonstration of the power of God, and a series of miracles, Ahab, egged on by Jezebel, set out to kill the prophet. And Elijah, who had so far been so brave, took refuge in flight. There follows the well-known story of his journey for forty days through the desert, his resting in the cave, and the unforgettable meeting between Elijah and God, who was found in the still small voice. But then this God, so terrible in his public revelation, so tender towards his prophet, invests the prophet with a task he obviously cannot execute (1 Kings 19:15-18). Elijah says, "I, even I only, am left." All the faithful have been slain, God has been rejected, and now "they seek my life, to take it away," and I shall soon be dead too.

But the Lord of hosts replies: "Go, return on your way to the wilderness of Damascus; and when you arrive, you shall anoint Hazael to be king over Syria; and Jehu the son of Nimshi you shall anoint to be king over Israel; and Elisha the son of Shaphat of Abel-meholah you shall anoint to be prophet in your place. And him who escapes from the sword of Hazael shall Jehu slay; and him who escapes from the sword of Jehu shall Elisha slay. Yet I will leave seven thousand in Israel, all the knees that have not bowed to Baal. . . ." This, then, is Yahweh's answer. He does not intervene again to save his prophet. He does not console him directly, although he certainly does so indirectly by sustaining him and showing him his love. He does not confirm him in his abdication and withdrawal. On the contrary, he gives to this despairing, defeated, and solitary man a superhuman and in some degree incomprehensible task. But this task is related to what Elijah himself has proclaimed. The judgment which God has pronounced rests on the whole people. The people has rejected God and broken the covenant. Very well, then; it will be broken too. An external enemy will defeat Israel. And what war spares, revolution will destroy; the division of the people into parties and factions will shatter Israel. Thus disaster is announced, but in the very announcement there is also a promise and a consolation, the seven thousand men, the remnant, for no matter what Elijah believes there is still a remnant, there are still true believers, in

Israel. And we should always remember that "seven" is the number of totality.

The remnant which is saved is thus the totality of Israel. There is ambiguity here. On the one hand the seven thousand *represent* the whole people (*pars pro toto*), so that the people as a whole is virtually saved by inclusion in the seven thousand. But on the other hand the seven thousand *are* the totality of the people, the rest are not Israel, and these remain the Israel of God in its fulness. We do not have to decide between the two meanings. We have simply to remember once more that when God rejects and condemns, when his strictness seems most absolute, he conjoins it at once with the announcing of his salvation and pardon—the two are indissolubly related. Judgment and grace are affirmed in the same movement. But this is not the theme of our present meditation. A remarkable point is that the task which God lays on the shoulders of Elijah is a political task. He is ordered to bring about a *coup d'état* in Damascus and then another *coup d'état* in Samaria. This prophetic command seems to be purely and simply political. Even more surprising is the fact that in reality Elijah does not do what he is ordered to do except as regards Elisha. The text goes on directly to tell us that Elijah departed and then met Elisha. He covered Elisha in his mantle, the sign of his power and also of his total person, so that from this moment Elisha is his successor, a continuation of the person of Elijah. Apart from designating the new prophet, Elijah does not do any of the things he was commanded. He does not go to Damascus, he does not nominate Hazael, nor does he nominate Jehu. On the contrary, the condemnation which God has passed on Ahab and the people of Israel seems to be ineffective.

Historians all agree today that the reign of Ahab was one of glory and power. The text itself shows this. After God's judgment Ahab wins his greatest victories over Syria. Militarily and politically Israel becomes a great people.

Ben-hadad is twice defeated. He has to restore all the towns he had taken from Israel. He has to accept the permanent presence of Israelites in Damascus, where the streets are reserved for them. Even more strangely, it is God himself who announces these victories to Ahab through his prophets (1 Kings 20:13). But the text also states that the army of Israel consisted of seven thousand men (v. 15). And perhaps everything depends on the fact that the Israel of God which would not bow the knee to Baal also numbered seven thousand. However that may be, the king is successful in both war and politics. He can live at ease, and the condemnation passed on him seems very light. But he commits an error. He makes an alliance with the king of Syria. He should really have put him to death according to God's command. He disobeys the ban.

We thus have here a strange contradiction. Elijah is given the task of staging the *coup d'état* in Syria which will replace Ben-hadad with Hazael, but God also considered that Ahab himself should have killed Ben-hadad. It is as though God was wanting to bring out the association between king and prophet. The king, a destructive conqueror, was supposed to slay his enemy according to the customs of war, but he certainly could not choose his successor. The prophet had no power at all to put the king of Syria to death, but he was given a positive order, the nomination of his successor. But this is immaterial, for what God expects does not take place at all. Ben-hadad is not put to death by Ahab and Hazael is not anointed by Elijah. Why does Elijah hold back? Surely it is inconceivable that he should not do what God commands. What is he waiting for? We do not know. The story as it goes on seems to suggest that God's condemnation is without effect. Israel is in the ascendant and it survives even the notorious Naboth incident. Did this have to come first? But even this did not trigger the revolution. For after Elijah accused Ahab, the king repented, humbled himself before

God, acknowledged the true God, and this time seriously. At once the Word of God came to Elijah: You have seen him repent? Very well, in these conditions judgment is temporarily lifted. The chastisement will not fall while Ahab lives. This, then, is what God was waiting for: the repentance of the worst king of Israel. This is why the course of events was delayed. Several golden years were given to Ahab while his repentance and conversion were awaited, and then three more years of peace. Then, his repentance being confirmed, Ahab, as he knew in advance, could die in his last battle. Thus the secret history of God remains secret. Time changes nothing. The judgment is still in force, but suspended for how many years? five or six in the reign of Ahab, two in the reign of Ahaziah, and then another five in the reign of Joram, another son of Ahab. During this whole period the formal and explicit order given to Elijah is not repeated. Elijah does not see the execution of the solemn order and the judgment pronounced in the desert. His role seems to be greatly reduced in the closing stages of Ahab's reign and in that of Ahaziah. Other prophets now speak to Ahab, especially Micaiah. Elijah intervenes only twice, first with the great prophecy regarding Naboth, and then with the prophecy of the death of Ahaziah. Elijah is then taken up without having done what he was commanded to do, and perhaps he always had the burden of this delay on his heart. Many more years will then pass after the translation of Elijah before Elisha does what his master was ordered to do. It does not seem that the order was given expressly to Elisha or that it was renewed. Probably Elijah himself passed it on to Elisha as a Word of God to be fulfilled. The fact that Elisha will execute it obviously implies a continuation of ministry. What God has said to one prophet may be done by another. Their work is complementary. We are naturally reminded of the words of Paul: "I planted, Apollos watered, but God gave the growth" (1 Corinthians 3:6). It is always hard for us to understand to what degree we are incorporated together into Christ by the act and decision of God, so that in God's plan our actions are complementary and necessary to one another.

Incidentally, the delay in the prophecy, and the fact that it was Elisha who finally carried out the order given to Elijah, raises inevitably a problem for modern criticism. The schema of a full-scale historical orientation is well known. The biblical authors, being religious, have supposedly imposed a pattern of religious interpretation on the reality of historical facts. They have tried to show that God was the master of events, that he directed history, that he rewarded the good, and so on. If in some degree a simplistic view of this kind might perhaps be discerned in Chronicles, the same certainly cannot be said here. If the religious authors really wanted to impose a religious interpretation on the historical facts, why did they do it so badly that nothing hangs together? Why did they say that the order was given to Elijah and then for ten or twelve years nothing was done? Why did they not just say that God spoke directly to Elisha and the latter obeyed? Is not this much more satisfying for simple minds? Why say specifically that condemnation is passed on Ahab and then go on to stress his victories? It would have been so much easier to omit this "invention," a command given to Elijah. Again, why is it that Ahab is defeated and slain after repenting? Why, according to the prophecy, does God say that his Word will be fulfilled in the reign of Ahab's son (1 Kings 21:29) when nothing takes place during the reign of his first son, Ahaziah, and the prophecy is not fulfilled? It would surely have been very simple to arrange things in such a way that everything fitted properly if, after all, these prophecies, these words of God, these divine interventions in history, are all the religious interpretations of pious authors. Did they really have to be so clumsy, so stupid, so simple, that they could not present a coherent

79

account or clear interpretation, but left things so muddled and ambiguous? But this very point gives us reason to ask whether by chance the simplicity and superficiality are not on the side of our critical historians and their rationalistic or agnostic interpretation of a history which is much more complex and difficult and profound, and in which after all God may have something to say. If only critical historians could advance their ideas as mere hypotheses instead of being so dogmatic!

However that may be, Elisha leaves for Damascus. No reason is given. Why does he do so at this juncture? No express sign has been given him by God. The time is no doubt favorable. There is an interval of peace between Samaria and Damascus. But it is evident that Elisha himself chooses his moment and takes the initiative in fulfilling this day the word that had been spoken to Elijah. It is the day he himself adjudges to be favorable. I think we shall have to speak of a calculated opportunism. It is incontestably left to Elisha's assessment, and he makes his assessment from a political perspective. Now is the time to thrust the sharp sword of God's act into the course of politics. But once the decision is made by Elisha according to the light he has, fortuitous circumstances are the direct occasion of the events that follow. The king of Syria is ill and appeals expressly to Elisha. He knows him to be the man of God. This is not surprising, for we recall that this king had Naaman beside him as his first officer. He has no doubt heard Naaman speak of him in a way that carried conviction. He knows what is going on. He thus appeals to the man of God to tell him what the result will be. He perhaps hopes that Elisha will heal him from a distance as in the case of Naaman. But instead we find a strange intermingling of motives and causes. The appeal to Elisha will be instead the cause of the king's death. Elisha is the bearer of healing to the one and of death to the other. For we now find a new coincidence. The messenger chosen by the king to go to Elisha is the very man who has been nominated as the new king of Syria. We thus have the impression that in fortuitous circumstances it is God who is manifested in the coincidences. It is he who combines things so that the clear and independent decisions of men obviously work together: the decision of Elisha to come to Damascus and the decision of the king to appeal to the prophet. We could hardly be wider of the mark than if we were to say that these human acts are electronically controlled by God. Their cause and their specific meaning are to be found in man and his situation.

Elisha now sets the political events in train by the very ambiguity of his saying. The healing of the king? The question of his illness? "Go, say to him, 'You shall certainly recover.' " This is the message for the king. The sickness which has struck him is not a fatal one. He will not die of it. Basically we should not take offense at the saying but we should accept it as a word of consolation that Elisha sends to the king.

As regards the precise matter which troubles the king, he may be reassured, and truly so, for what Elisha tells him is God's assurance. Hypocrisy? No, for while what he says to the king is undoubtedly limited, the limitation is imposed by the king's own attitude. Ben-hadad has consulted him as a diviner, a magician. All this is clearly at the level of magic and the king is exclusively preoccupied with his illness. God is ready to let himself be consulted at the level of magic too; we have plenty of other examples of this acceptance by God of man's errors in this area, primarily the Urim and Thummim. And when man consults him at this level he will be given an answer at precisely the same level. An ambiguous reply is given to a magical question. A strictly limited reply is given to a strictly limited question. "Is this illness fatal?" "No"—that is all. But there is a further message for Hazael: "The Lord has shown me that he shall certainly die." The messenger, who no doubt does not understand the contradiction, does not ask anything. But Elisha knows God's decision. He is seized by sorrow for his people. Faced by Elisha's tears, Hazael now has a question. Elisha acts as God's prophet in telling Hazael what he will do, what God has decided he will be: the scourge of Israel. "I know the evil that you will do. . . ." Elisha describes to him the atrocities of war. When he hears it, Hazael is greatly surprised. He does not understand it at all. He is not one of the great commanders of Syria. He has no hope, humanly speaking, of doing what Elisha declares to him.

"How . . . could I do this great thing?" This naive question has two aspects. It shows first the good faith of Hazael. He has no idea what is meant. In other words, he has not been involved in any conspiracy. He has no intention of becoming king. He has no thought of seizing power. Thus it is truly God's Word which triggers the event, which sets in train what follows. The other aspect of the naivety of Hazael is that he thinks Elisha is telling him a great thing. Elisha has been speaking of evil, of the horrors of war, and Hazael evidently regards it as a great thing. In effect, even in times of peace defeating Israel was very much on the minds of the Syrians, the traditional enemies of Israel. Dashing to pieces Israel's children and ripping up the pregnant women was indeed a great thing. This Hazael is an admirable specimen of the natural man, very innocent and very simple. To Hazael's question Elisha replies with God's Word, which is both precise and also ambiguous: "The Lord has shown me that you are to be king over Syria." This is clear enough. But the rest is obscure, namely, the "how" and the "when." Here we are back at the level of human decisions. Elisha, the man of God, tells this messenger what he *is* (what he actually will be) before God, just as he told the unbelieving officer of Israel what he was (what he would be) before God. But to speak this word, to intimate the actual death of Ben-hadad and the kingship of Hazael, is no easy thing for the prophet. To be sure, he has only to speak (and we shall return to this limitation). But this word is harder to speak, more difficult to formulate, more implicating for his being, more binding for his life, than any great act, even a miracle, could ever be. For this word is spoken against his own wishes. Here again we can see clearly three possible positions. There is first the pure and simple mechanization of man by God, who moves him like a pawn. Then there is the willing obedience of man at any cost to the Word of God spoken to him, an obedience which may sometimes be in accord with the will, desire, intelligence, and choice of man, so that man is full of joy (this will be the situation in the kingdom), but which may also clash with the will, desires, intelligence, and choices of man, so that there is great sorrow as in Gethsemane.

Finally, the third position is that man makes his own decision without any knowledge of God's intention. Now all the stories make it plain that the first hypothesis can be ruled out completely. If thus far we have seen Elisha in agreement with God, he is still obedient now, but this time in pain, sacrifice, and confusion. Elisha weeps; in his faith and obedience to the Word of God he cannot do anything but speak it. It is by a free decision that he obeys, yet it is against his own will, for he is horrified by the future which he triggers. It is against the love he has for his own people. We have seen already from the story of the siege of Samaria that he does not isolate himself completely from this people, and especially not when the disaster seems to be so gratuitous and without cause, for the people is not now rebellious or in revolt.

Elisha is well aware of this. There is also in Judah a truly good and pious king. Elisha is not told to preach divine chastisement in Israel nor to issue a call for repentance. Nevertheless, catastrophe draws near. Elisha weeps and yet he obeys, pronouncing God's design. He submits to this incomprehensible decision, and, as a figure of Jesus Christ, he weeps even as he submits to this condemnation. For he and his people are one. It is he who invests Hazael with the power which will allow the conqueror to assassinate both his people and his king. "You would have no power over me unless it had been given you from above" (John 19:11). Elisha does not differentiate himself from his people. But this trial which God has willed must be endured.

The word of Elisha to Hazael is ambiguous: "He shall certainly die. . . ." "You shall do much evil to the children of Israel. . . ." "You are to be king over Syria." From this point on man can be allowed to follow his own inclinations. In the eyes of Hazael the word Elisha spoke was not a Word of God. Certainly the prophet spoke twice on the Lord's behalf, but Hazael had no cause to hear it as a Word of the true God. It is not in obedience to God that he sets to work. What has been said to him, the possibility of becoming king and of eventual glory, is enough to get things moving. Power is put in his hands. All that is now needed is the covetousness which will stir up ambition, the thirst for power, the appetite for renown.[1]

There is no need to point the way. The suggestion is enough. The ambiguous saying is not ambiguous to Hazael. His sin fulfils God's will for evil even though God does not command it. All that God does is to lay a simple possibility before man, to open a gate, and to let things develop of themselves. He allows covetousness to rise up in Hazael, and this is all that is needed.

We learn from this two lessons. The first is that in the political context (and we do not have our sights on more than this) God has his Word brought by a man. It is only a human word addressed to men who do not believe. God

---

[1] In passing, the name of the king, Ben-hadad, should be noted. It refers to the god Hadad, to whom was attributed the title of Baal (lord). The god Hadad, who is compared to a bull, causes his voice to be heard in the thunder and dispenses rain. He is lord and procreator (Dussaud, *Mythologie phénicienne*). Nevertheless, there is no religious motive for Elisha's action. It is not that the God of Israel is joining battle with the son of Hadad. There is no question of guaranteeing true religion by the murder of the king. And what makes this clear with grim humor is that the son of Hazael will in turn bear the name of Ben-hadad.

does not accompany the word with any manifestation of glory or power. This simple word at the everyday level is neither indisputable nor imperative. At no point is man bound to it. God does not work in the heart of Hazael. He simply puts him before the Word. The Word is not a commandment. Hazael might do something very different from what is suggested. God has not traced out an implacable future in which the poor king is involved with no power at all to change anything. He might challenge this word which is spoken to him by a man like himself. The word is not irreducible. He might construe it very differently. For it is ambiguous. Hazael is not a poor figure of a king subjected to an ineluctable fate. It is for him to choose what he will do. It is within his own autonomy and independence that he will undertake to seize power and conquer kingdoms. It seems to me that this situation is a good illustration. The church never has to formulate a commandment of God in relation to political power, which in principle cannot recognize God as the true God. It has never to say to the state: This must be done. It has rather to tell it on God's behalf what will in effect be done, what the state on its own initiative will undoubtedly be led to do. It has to be a prophet then? In a sense, yes. But serious meditation before God, dispassionate and disinterested understanding in God, should allow it to have a good knowledge of developments. A dispassionate stance is always indispensable, for action or taking sides inevitably veils the significance of the future. This leads us to another aspect of the text. The prophet speaks and that is all. He does not act. He announces this Word of God, but he does not have to make it efficacious or effective. He speaks, and men and events are charged with a kind of force or passion or weight. But the prophet does not lead Hazael. The text does not even say that he "anoints" him king. He gives him no counsel. Just as he does not bear arms in the siege of Samaria, he does not intervene in Damascus, e.g., by forming a group of supporters around Hazael. There is no action to take. Once the Word of God is pronounced he does not have to undertake to do it. He does not have to have a hand in its fulfilment. He does not have to find specific ways of giving it effect; men will see to this themselves. He does not have to demonstrate the efficaciousness of this Word as such. Man is set before it as before a very hard object against which he dashes himself. Now the prophet retires from the scene. The reality of political action is no concern of his. Once Hazael is set moving, he may be trusted to do the rest. He sets out to kill the king, and he himself finds the means to do it without difficulty. He will then reign for half a century and will in effect devastate the people of God. He begins in the territories across the Jordan, which he ravages and annexes. He then marches across all Israel and wounds Joram the king (8:28). He conquers Samaria, destroys its army, overthrows Jehu, and completely subjugates his son Jehoahaz. He leaves in Israel only ten chariots and fifty horsemen, "for the king of Syria had destroyed them and made them like the dust at threshing" (13:7). He also attacks the southern kingdom of Judah. He takes and destroys one of the principal fortresses, that of Gath (12:17). He then attacks Jerusalem. Now at the time there is a good and pious king in Jerusalem, namely, Jehoash, but he is defeated. Jerusalem is besieged, and astonishingly the king is ready to pay a tribute in order to save the city. But this is set so high that the royal treasury cannot meet it and the temple treasury has to be raided, "all the votive gifts that Jehoshaphat and Jehoram and Ahaziah, his fathers, had dedicated," "all the treasuries in the house of the Lord." It is on these conditions that Hazael goes away from Jerusalem. In other words, the evil done by the king of Syria is not just political and military. He also desecrates all that is considered most holy. He profanes the divinely instituted cultus. This undoubtedly signifies that God no longer supports the cultus, that he no longer accepts the consecration of cultic objects.

The people has disobeyed too much; it has been too much a "religious" people; it has been too much like other peoples and not itself, the holy people. What is the good of maintaining the cultus and holy things if the people itself is not holy? God manifests in practice his refusal of the worship of this people, and he manifests it by means of this conqueror.

Yet we also find the same recoil as upon the Assyrians. It is not enough for the man who does evil to be able to say: "God has sent me; God wills it; God has prompted it." The scourge of God is still a scourge. The evil it does is still evil before God, and God judges. There is judgment again on the very instrument of God's wrath. This "instrument" is in truth responsible. In the presence of God's Word, which does not constrain, he has chosen to be the scourge of God. Amos, another prophet, announces the punishment of Hazael: "For three transgressions of Damascus, and for four, I will not revoke the punishment; because they have threshed Gilead with threshing sledges of iron. So I will send a fire upon the house of Hazael . . . and the people of Israel shall go into exile to Kir," says the Lord (Amos 1:3-5). God is the master of Hazael too. What is contrary to his love for men and for his people is always something God condemns. Hazael cannot plead ignorance that all this is evil. Elisha told him of all the evil he would do. There can be no ambiguity in this regard. And it is again the role of the prophet and the church to show what is bad. But what God tells Hazael is bad he regards as a great thing. From the political standpoint it is in fact a great thing. Political passion causes him to forget that it is all under condemnation. He surrenders to the glory of great political achievements. Thus God is manifested not merely as he who is King of kings and Master of nations but also as he who behind historical success and grandeur issues judgments and fixes the final end.

Note should undoubtedly be taken of the exposition of the Amos passage by Neher. His translation of verse 3 reads: "For three transgressions . . . I will not answer." God will not answer this people. He does not merely judge it; he refuses to talk to it. For, he says, these peoples are in God's kingdom by reason of the covenant. Alongside the covenant with Israel there is a universal covenant based on the Noachic covenant, and all nations are the beneficiaries of this. These peoples are now threatened by a new divine scourge, each in turn. Syria has been the scourge of God, and now the Assyrian assumes the role. These peoples, headed by Syria, turn to God, perhaps appealing to him, Hazael and his house after him. But now God will not answer them. "The silence of God reveals the existence of sin." Hazael has not just committed any sin. He has actually transgressed the covenant. God will not speak any more, and "history will speak the language of God." As Israel and Judah have been delivered into the hands of history, so it will now be with Syria. The glory of Hazael will be quickly tarnished. The Word of God which launched him will be spoken no more when he invokes it.

Subject at last to this judgment, Hazael must die after a glorious reign of half a century. The story is a gripping one (1 Kings 13:14). Joash, a bad king, is now reigning in Israel. He does what is evil in the sight of the Lord. It is said of him, as of Jehoahaz, that he continues the sin of Jeroboam. This sin of Jeroboam is often recalled, and it is of political importance, for it means using God to enhance the state (we shall examine the significance of this later). Here, then, is the sin that Joash commits again. Nevertheless, he recognizes that Elisha is a prophet, a man of God, of the true God. Thus, when he hears that Elisha is dying, he goes to him and weeps. He perceives that if there is protection for Israel he does not owe it to the golden calves but to Elisha, in whom he discerns the true grandeur of God, real power, "the chariots of Israel and its horsemen." Elisha is of more value to Israel than all its armies.

There is great merit in the fact that Joash realized this, for during the years of Israel's defeat Elisha must have seemed to be the prophet of a false god, as under Joram. But Joash, torn by conflicting impulses, even calls Elisha "my father," and Elisha cannot resist this appeal. He replies and gives the assurance of deliverance. He has the king perform symbolical acts, and the remarkable thing is that the king obeys without demur: "Take a bow and arrows"; "Open the window eastward"; "Draw the bow." The king does all these things. Then the prophet puts his hands on the king's hands as he holds the taut bow. Symbolically this means that the prophet transmits his power as a man of God to the king. Joash has recognized that Elisha is the chariots of Israel and its horsemen. He is more Israel's king than the king himself. He is the incarnation of true royalty. He is the true bulwark of Israel. In response to this confession, the prophet confers his strength on the king.

"Shoot." The king obeys, and this arrow, shot towards Damascus, is the prophetic sign which Elisha then interprets: "The Lord's arrow of victory." God's decision is now taken. The Lord will now be merciful. He remembers his covenant. He has compassion. The test is now over and Syria's role is at an end. This is God's global decision. But there is more to come. Elisha says again to the king: "Take the arrows," and: "Strike the ground with them." The king obeys without any attempt to understand and by chance he strikes three times. This arouses in Elisha a last spurt of anger: "You should have struck five or six times; then you would have struck down Syria until you had made an end of it, but now you will strike down Syria only three times." Here we see again the strange combination of God's decision and man's initiative. God has made known his will to the prophet and now the king of Israel will accomplish God's work, but according to his own means, decisions, and resources. The king is granted liberty to strike the ground twice, three times, five times, as often as he likes; if he stops, it is by his own choice. This will be the measure of his action, which otherwise would be without measure within the good will of God. In fact, military fortunes change and the bad king Joash recaptures all the cities of Israel from Syria.

On the point of death Elisha announces both the end of the trial and also the death of Hazael. Hazael seems to be closely bound up with the existence and presence of Elisha. The prophet provided the spur which brought him to the throne and the prophet now brings about his fall and death, as though the power of Hazael were linked to the presence of Elisha. Nor is it hard to understand this. During the whole of the long life of Elisha Israel is under constant trial. It moves from defeat to famine and from revolution to massacre. The hand of God is heavy upon it at this time. Chastisement follows chastisement. But it should always be remembered that God does not strike without healing, that he does not condemn without consoling, that he does not judge without the gospel. During these seventy years of testing Elisha is there.

Elisha is the visible and active presence of God himself. At every instant he carries consolation for the poor and afflicted. He is the constantly renewed miracle of an incarnate Word. He can grant consolation to the people in every crisis, for he is the sign and proof and witness that God has not abandoned his people. The test can be terrible but the prophet is there, and for those who have eyes to see and ears to hear this is enough. Even if the prophet does not change events, the fulness of God is a sufficient answer. The same seems to be true of the church, the body of Christ. Perhaps it does not have to intervene directly in politics. But its presence is enough to make the worst disasters endurable. And perhaps because Christ has said: "I am with you always, to the close of the age" (Matthew 28:20), the history of the last times can only be a series of disasters from the human standpoint, as the Gospels and Peter and Revelation intimate. Because Christ has come and is always present there can be no progress in the achieving of human happiness.

But now Elisha is dying. The consolation of Israel, the clear indication of God's power, is being taken from it. So the trial ends. It is more than Israel can bear. God arrests the disasters lest his people, left on its own, should be destroyed spiritually. "He will not let you be tempted beyond your strength" (1 Corinthians 10:13). Yes, Jehu, Hazael, the great destroyers, can arise and are unleashed only when God has provided and sent and set in place the one who consoles and whose presence can make up things for man beyond all he dare hope. Now that Elisha is no more, Israel will have respite. The time of testing and judgment is over. Under the rule of bad, crafty, proud, and idolatrous kings (Joash, Jeroboam, Menahem), Israel will for a period recover its glory, supremacy, and political liberty, and will live in the illusion of its own power and reconstituted glory until the final collapse and deportation.

Historians who think the history told in the Bible is pious and distorted ought to ask themselves why it is that these biblical historians who supposedly want to prove something always tell us about the disasters under good kings and the victories under idolatrous kings. For us, the question is that of the respite which can be granted to a people, the growth of its material prosperity, its glory, its tranquillity, its culture. Satan has fallen from heaven to earth like a flash of lightning because the Son of Man is the Son of God.

The respite of peace should be for us a warning to greater watchfulness and to greater love.

IV

Jehu

2 Kings 9-10

1 Then Elisha the prophet called one of the sons of the prophets and said to him, "Gird up your loins, and take this flask of oil in your hand, and go to Ramoth-gilead. 2 And when you arrive, look there for Jehu the son of Jehoshaphat, son of Nimshi; and go in and bid him rise from among his fellows, and lead him to an inner chamber. 3 Then take the flask of oil, and pour it on his head, and say, 'Thus says the Lord, I anoint you king over Israel.' Then open the door and flee; do not tarry."

4 So the young man, the prophet, went to Ramoth-gilead. 5 And when he came, behold, the commanders of the army were in council; and he said, "I have an errand to you, O commander." And Jehu said, "To which of us all?" And he said, "To you, O commander." 6 So he arose, and went into the house; and the young man poured the oil on his head, saying to him, "Thus says the Lord the God of Israel, I anoint you king over the people of the Lord, over Israel. 7 And you shall strike down the house of Ahab your master, that I may avenge on Jezebel the blood of my servants the prophets, and the blood of all the servants of the Lord. 8 For the whole house of Ahab shall perish; and I will cut off from Ahab every male, bond or free, in Israel. 9 And I will make the house of Ahab like the house of Jeroboam the son of Nebat, and like the house of Baasha the son of Ahijah. 10 And the dogs shall eat Jezebel in the territory of Jezreel, and none shall bury her." Then he opened the door, and fled.

11 When Jehu came out to the servants of his master, they said to him, "Is all well?" And he said to them, "You know the fellow and his talk." 12 And they said, "That is not true; tell us now." And he said, "Thus and so he spoke to me, saying, 'Thus says the Lord, I anoint you king over Israel.' " 13 Then in haste every man

of them took his garment, and put it under him on the bare steps, and they blew the trumpet, and proclaimed, "Jehu is king."

14 Thus Jehu the son of Jehoshaphat the son of Nimshi conspired against Joram. (Now Joram with all Israel had been on guard at Ramoth-gilead against Hazael king of Syria; 15 but King Joram had returned to be healed in Jezreel of the wounds which the Syrians had given him, when he fought with Hazael king of Syria.) So Jehu said, "If this is your mind, then let no one slip out of the city to go and tell the news in Jezreel." 16 Then Jehu mounted his chariot, and went to Jezreel, for Joram lay there. And Ahaziah king of Judah had come down to visit Joram.

17 Now the watchman was standing on the tower in Jezreel, and he spied the company of Jehu as he came, and said, "I see a company." And Joram said, "Take a horseman, and send to meet them, and let him say, 'Is it peace?' " 18 So a man on horseback went to meet him, and said, "Thus says the king, 'Is it peace?' " And Jehu said, "What have you to do with peace? Turn round and ride behind me." And the watchman reported, saying, "The messenger reached them, but he is not coming back." 19 Then he sent out a second horseman, who came to them and said, "Thus the king has said, 'Is it peace?' " And Jehu answered, "What have you to do with peace? Turn round and ride behind me." 20 Again the watchman reported, "He reached them, but he is not coming back. And the driving is like the driving of Jehu the son of Nimshi; for he drives furiously."

21 Joram said, "Make ready." And they made ready his chariot. Then Joram king of Israel and Ahaziah king of Judah set out, each in his chariot, and met him at the property of Naboth the Jezreelite. 22 And when Joram saw Jehu, he said, "Is it peace, Jehu?" He answered, "What peace can there be, so long as the harlotries and the sorceries of your mother Jezebel are so many?" 23 Then Joram reined about and fled, saying to Ahaziah, "Treachery, O Ahaziah." 24 And Jehu drew his bow with his full strength, and shot Joram between the shoulders, so that the arrow pierced his heart, and he sank in his chariot. 25 Jehu said to Bidkar his aide, "Take him up, and cast him on the plot of ground belonging to Naboth the Jezreelite; for remember when you and I rode side by side behind Ahab his father, how the Lord uttered this oracle against him: 26 'As surely as I saw yesterday the blood of Naboth and the blood of his sons—says the Lord—I will requite you on this plot of ground.' Now therefore take him up and cast him on the plot of ground, in accordance with the word of the Lord."

27 When Ahaziah the king of Judah saw this, he fled in the direction of Beth-haggan. And Jehu pursued him, and said, "Shoot him also"; and they shot him in the chariot at the ascent of Gur, which is by Ibleam. And he fled to Megiddo, and died there. 28 His servants carried him in a chariot to Jerusalem, and buried him in his tomb with his fathers in the city of David.

29 In the eleventh year of Joram the son of Ahab, Ahaziah began to reign over Judah.

30 When Jehu came to Jezreel, Jezebel heard of it; and she painted her eyes, and adorned her head, and looked out of the window. 31 And as Jehu entered the gate, she said, "Is it peace, you Zimri, murderer of your master?" 32 And he lifted up his face to the window, and said, "Who is on my side? Who?" Two or three eunuchs looked out at him. 33 He said, "Throw her down." So they threw her down; and some of her blood spattered on the wall and on the horses, and they trampled on her. 34 Then he went in and ate and drank; and he said, "See now to this cursed woman, and bury her; for she is a king's daughter." 35 But when they went to bury her, they found no more of her than the skull and the feet and the palms of her hands. 36 When they came back and told him, he said, "This is the word of the Lord, which he spoke by his servant Elijah the Tishbite, 'In the territory of Jezreel the dogs shall eat the flesh of Jezebel; 37 and the corpse of Jezebel shall be as dung upon the face of the field in the territory of Jezreel, so that no one can say, This is Jezebel.' "

1 Now Ahab had seventy sons in Samaria. So Jehu wrote letters, and sent them to Samaria, to the rulers of the city, to the elders, and to the guardians of the sons of Ahab, saying, 2 "Now then, as soon as this letter comes to you, seeing your master's sons are with you, and there are with you chariots and horses, fortified cities also, and weapons, 3 select the best and fittest of your master's sons and set him on his father's throne, and fight for your master's house." 4 But they were exceedingly afraid, and said, "Behold, the two kings could not stand before him; how then can we stand?" 5 So he who was over the palace, and he who was over the city, together with the elders and the guardians, sent to Jehu, saying, "We are your servants, and we will do all that you bid us. We will not make any one king; do whatever is good in your eyes." 6 Then he wrote to them a second letter, saying, "If you are on my side, and if you are ready to obey me, take the heads of your master's sons, and come to me at Jezreel tomorrow at this time." Now the king's sons, seventy

persons, were with the great men of the city, who were bringing them up. 7 And when the letter came to them, they took the king's sons, and slew them, seventy persons, and put their heads in baskets, and sent them to him at Jezreel. 8 When the messenger came and told him, "They have brought the heads of the king's sons," he said, "Lay them in two heaps at the entrance of the gate until the morning." 9 Then in the morning, when he went out, he stood, and said to all the people, "You are innocent. It was I who conspired against my master, and slew him; but who struck down all these? 10 Know then that there shall fall to the earth nothing of the word of the Lord, which the Lord spoke concerning the house of Ahab; for the Lord has done what he said by his servant Elijah." 11 So Jehu slew all that remained of the house of Ahab in Jezreel, all his great men, and his familiar friends, and his priests, until he left him none remaining.

12 Then he set out and went to Samaria. On the way, when he was at Beth-eked of the Shepherds, 13 Jehu met the kinsmen of Ahaziah king of Judah, and he said, "Who are you?" And they answered, "We are the kinsmen of Ahaziah, and we came down to visit the royal princes and the sons of the queen mother." 14 And he said, "Take them alive." And they took them alive, and slew them at the pit of Beth-eked, forty-two persons, and he spared none of them.

15 And when he departed from there, he met Jehonadab the son of Rechab coming to meet him; and he greeted him, and said to him, "Is your heart true to my heart as mine is to yours?" And Jehonadab answered, "It is." Jehu said, "If it is, give me your hand." So he gave him his hand. And Jehu took him up with him into the chariot. 16 And he said, "Come with me, and see my zeal for the Lord." So he had him ride in his chariot. 17 And when he came to Samaria, he slew all that remained to Ahab in Samaria, till he had wiped them out, according to the word of the Lord which he spoke to Elijah.

18 Then Jehu assembled all the people, and said to them, "Ahab served Baal a little; but Jehu will serve him much. 19 Now therefore call to me all the prophets of Baal, all his worshipers and all his priests; let none be missing, for I have a great sacrifice to offer to Baal; whoever is missing shall not live." But Jehu did it with cunning in order to destroy the worshipers of Baal. 20 And Jehu ordered, "Sanctify a solemn assembly for Baal." So they proclaimed it. 21 And Jehu sent throughout all Israel; and all the worshipers of Baal came, so that there was not a man left who did not come. And

they entered the house of Baal, and the house of Baal was filled from one end to the other. 22 He said to him who was in charge of the wardrobe, "Bring out the vestments for all the worshipers of Baal." So he brought out the vestments for them. 23 Then Jehu went into the house of Baal with Jehonadab the son of Rechab; and he said to the worshipers of Baal, "Search, and see that there is no servant of the Lord here among you, but only the worshipers of Baal." 24 Then he went in to offer sacrifices and burnt offerings.

Now Jehu had stationed eighty men outside, and said, "The man who allows any of those whom I give into your hands to escape shall forfeit his life." 25 So as soon as he had made an end of offering the burnt offering, Jehu said to the guard and to the officers, "Go in and slay them; let not a man escape." So when they put them to the sword, the guard and the officers cast them out and went into the inner room of the house of Baal 26 and they brought out the pillar that was in the house of Baal, and burned it. 27 And they demolished the pillar of Baal, and demolished the house of Baal, and made it a latrine to this day.

28 Thus Jehu wiped out Baal from Israel. 29 But Jehu did not turn aside from the sins of Jeroboam the son of Nebat, which he made Israel to sin, the golden calves that were in Bethel, and in Dan. 30 And the Lord said to Jehu, "Because you have done well in carrying out what is right in my eyes, and have done to the house of Ahab all that was in my heart, your sons of the fourth generation shall sit on the throne of Israel." 31 But Jehu was not careful to walk in the law of the Lord the God of Israel with all his heart; he did not turn from the sins of Jeroboam, which he made Israel to sin.

32 In those days the Lord began to cut off parts of Israel. Hazael defeated them throughout the territory of Israel: 33 from the Jordan eastward, all the land of Gilead, the Gadites, and the Reubenites, and the Manassites, from Aroer, which is by the valley of the Arnon, that is, Gilead and Bashan. 34 Now the rest of the acts of Jehu, and all that he did, and all his might, are they not written in the Book of the Chronicles of the Kings of Israel? 35 So Jehu slept with his fathers, and they buried him in Samaria. And Jehoahaz his son reigned in his stead. 36 The time that Jehu reigned over Israel in Samaria was twenty-eight years.

Elisha now carries out the second part of the order given to Elijah. Having nominated Hazael, he anoints Jehu. He again engages in a very definite political action, and this one is also very dramatic and bloody. It is true enough that according to the prophecy those who escape Hazael fall under the sword of Jehu, but the work of these two scourges of God is not the same. Whereas Hazael ravages and slaughters the whole people of Israel and Judah, Jehu exterminates the political elite, all that is represented by Ahab.

I

In this second movement we shall find that Elisha's action has the same features. These may be briefly recalled. Elisha simply triggers the political action. He is at the starting-point. He makes a gesture and speaks a word which sets things going with the ineluctability of a machine. He is literally the finger that presses a button and the whole mechanism starts functioning. But then Elisha does not intervene again. He has no part at all in the political action. He does not counsel Jehu. He does not approve or disapprove. He has given a push and opened a door with his word, and then he steps aside and lets things happen. Even the word is remarkable ambiguous. Another point worth noting is that Elisha does not go to find Jehu as he did Hazael. He acts through an intermediary as in the case of Naaman. He sends a son of the prophets, a young man, a prophet's servant, perhaps a student in the prophetic schools that existed at the time. Elisha acts from a distance. He uses a mouthpiece. This may well mean, as I myself believe, that he is differentiating his action from that of magic. Elisha has often been accused of acting like a magician. It seems to me, however, that the Naaman incident, like this one, should serve to refute this interpretation.

The power which will be expressed does not reside in Elisha. It is not his person which heals or which makes kings. No intrinsic force guarantees what he says and does. Any servant can do as much, for the only task is to transmit a Word of God. Elisha simply knows that God's will is at issue, and he passes on this will. He does not use any sign or personal power. This is the point of the intermediary. Elisha is the mediator who causes what he knows to be an actual decision of God to be carried out by someone else. One is naturally reminded of the way Jesus acts through his disciples when they are sent to the towns of Judah, or the way Christ acts through his church—a confirmation of the fact that Elisha is a type of Jesus Christ. Now this very employment of an intermediary has a result one might expect. The message is changed. In the same way the Word spoken by God in Christ is undoubtedly modified by the church, and not for the better. What Elisha says to the young man is this: "Lead Jehu to an inner chamber, anoint him with the oil of kingship, and say to him, 'Thus says the Lord, I anoint you king over Israel,' then flee, do not tarry." There is nothing more, no address. The message to Jehu is both radical and also very terse. But this is not the way the young man delivers it. Instead of fleeing at once, he gives an address (as the church often does), and he adds on his own invention: "You shall strike down the house of Ahab. . . . I will avenge on Jezebel the blood of the prophets. . . . the whole house of Ahab shall perish, every male, bond or free. . . . The dogs shall eat Jezebel. . . ." In sum, the young man outlines a program of action for Jehu, which is something Elisha does not do. Now the young man is undoubtedly using prophecies of Elijah (1 Kings 21:19-24), but Elisha does not tell him to do this. It is on this false transmission that the whole career of Jehu is based. We are usually struck by the fierce and bloodthirsty character of Jehu, and this is clear enough. But another and no less decisive element should not be missed, namely, that all Jehu's work is done in a situation of ambiguity and misunderstanding.

He is anointed by God, but in the long run he does

nothing but evil wherever he goes. He fulfils prophecies, but he is condemned for so doing. He is a man of God, but he uses all the methods of the devil.

We are faced again by a question we have investigated already, that of the coincidence between God's design and man's, that of God's employment of what is bad in man to bring about what he himself wills. Here, for example, there is undoubtedly coincidence between the anointing of Jehu and the existence of a conspiracy among the generals of Joram's army. In fact, the conspiracy probably existed already. This would explain the immediate support of the generals and their siding with Jehu.

The situation was indeed favorable for a *coup d'état.* The army was in the field, the king was wounded and had withdrawn, and the generals had a free hand. Probably Jehu already wanted to seize power and the decision of God passed on by the young man seemed to him to be a sign for action. There is also an obvious coincidence between the work that Jehu is commissioned to do and the glimpses we catch of his temperament. He is clearly a bloodthirsty man, and this not merely by reason of his trade. He is at home in massacres, and we thus see God choosing as the agent of his judgment a man whose temperament corresponds to what is asked of him. If God's choice often falls on the most incapable, the one who humanly speaking is most remote from what he ordains, here the reverse holds true. And this demonstrates yet again the sovereign liberty of God in all his decisions and choices. Furthermore, when Jehu embarks on his series of massacres, he can undoubtedly say that he is fulfilling prophecies. But all the same his action is like that of any dictator after a *coup d'état.* It is the most elementary prudence to destroy and extirpate whatever is connected with the previous regime. The story is told in such a way that no divine will or prophecy plays any part. Nothing has to be changed. Jehu, a usurping general, kills the king and his family, his ministers and governors; he might equally well be Sulla or Hitler. There is thus full coincidence between the normal conduct of the usurper and the decision of God. It is through this normal conduct that the prophecy is fulfilled. On the other hand, a rationalist or unbeliever might well argue that the prophecy is a propagandist justification or ideological cover for the understandable acts of a usurper.

However that may be, Jehu fulfils all that is declared by Elijah's prophecy. He slays the family of Ahab, King Joram of Israel his son, King Ahaziah of Judah the son of Athaliah, who was a niece of Ahab, Jezebel of course, seventy other sons of Ahab, and the forty-two kinsmen of Ahaziah. He also slays those who have served Ahab, the governors and ministers, leading men and familiar friends resident in Jezreel, whom he accuses of having killed the seventy sons of Ahab. He thus slays all those who have claimed to be his supporters and servants (10:11). Then he slays the remaining politicians in Samaria (10:17). Finally he slays all the priests and worshipers of Baal. In perpetrating these massacres he claims to be fulfilling the prophecy he has heard against Ahab (9:25-26). And he is at pains to fulfil it deliberately and systematically in detail by ordering his officer to take the corpse of Joram and throw it in the field of Naboth, since Elijah had declared that this field would be the place where vengeance was executed. It may be seen that we are now in the presence of something quite different from what usually characterizes the fulfilment of prophecy. There seems to be here a kind of legalistic literalism. In fact Jehu commandeers the prophecy in order to fulfil it. But when the prophecy was first given it was not addressed to Jehu.

It was a general and in some sort objective prophecy. The young man, as we have seen, is the one who tells Jehu it is his task to fulfil this prophecy. This offers a further occasion to reflect on the prophecy. In relation to Ahab and his house it is certainly a judgment of God. But it does not seem to be an explicit order given to a specific man, to Jehu. In this history prophecy will often (though not always) be the announcing of what will happen. God condemns Ahab, and it comes about that his whole house is destroyed. The prophecy is a kind of description of a chain of historical events, but without implying either the express will of God in the event or God's approval of the one who undertakes to accomplish these events. The prophecy issued against Ahab describes the causal mechanism of evil and violence. When at a moment in history and in a given historical situation evil is initiated by a man or a group, it carries within it its own logic, impetus, and rigor. When evil is done it always introduces an element of ineluctability into human relations and conduct.

The idolatry of Ahab, his worship of bloodthirsty gods (demanding human sacrifices), the unleashing of magical forces by Jezebel, the violence of the king in the massacre of believers in Yahweh—all this sets in motion a logical sequence of events whose flame will finally blow back and consume Ahab himself. In sum, the prophecy seems to be a simple illustration of the teaching of Christ: "All who take the sword will perish by the sword" (Matthew 26:52). We have here both a divine judgment and also a mechanism of events. Undoubtedly Jehu is the man who executes what God has previously announced. In some sense he is the one who manages the important acts which accomplish the condemnation. But in the last resort he does it all in his own interests. He takes part in the fulfilment of the prophecy, but he does so, one might say, within the order of political logic. The prophecy intimates this unfolding of political logic. Ahab triggers the movement. Jehu, the champion of Yahweh, uses the same weapons as Ahab, the weapons of politics and violence. The chain of events will finally turn against Jehu too, as we shall see.

In this explanation there is no thought of diminishing

the importance of the prophecy, or of reducing it to simple foresight. One should remember, however, that every Word of God has several dimensions. One cannot say that prophecy is this or that. On the contrary, it is both this and also that. Thus in this vision of God's action there can be no question at all of cutting down God's sovereignty over history and events, but rather of showing that this sovereignty is multiple, supple, and living, not mechanical or metaphysical. God has condemned Ahab. God has chosen Jehu as king. But God leaves it to man to find ways and means. He leaves it to man to determine his acts himself in so far as he is responsible. God opens a door as it were, and the passion of man is unleashed.

One is irresistibly reminded of the great text of Zechariah: "The Lord says, I will cause men to fall each into the hand of his shepherd, and each into the hand of his king . . . and I will deliver none from their hand" (Zechariah 11:6). This is, in sum, the moment when God turns aside and veils his face. He lets man act according to what he is. We thus have a torrent of injustice, extirpation, and hate. To deliver man into the hands of man is the worst thing possible. This is the level we are at with Jehu. God has no need to inspire the heart of Jehu to bring about these atrocities. He has only to nominate him king and then let things take their course. The work of the bloodthirsty man is well done. When God lets men fall into the hands of other men, when his love no longer fights to prevent the historical outbreak of violence, the man of blood triumphs. The same significance attaches to the famous choice of David (2 Samuel 24) when in punishment God lets him choose between three scourges (famine, war, and pestilence), and David replies: "Let us fall into the hand of the Lord, for his mercy is great; but let me not fall into the hand of man." God is love even when he judges, condemns, and punishes; but there is nothing worse than unleashed man even when he wants to do the will of

God. Jehu is this unleashed man; he is unleashed when he is anointed king of Israel.

Jehu is a destroyer, this is clear. But let us also consider his other acts, the political devices he uses in relation to the seventy brothers of the king.

He begins by writing to the governors and ministers recommending that they should select a new king from among the heirs. He does not write as a usurper. But these politicians, knowing his power, refuse to do this, and submit to his orders. He then sends a second letter, which is a masterpiece of irony and ambiguity. The Hebrew text simply says: "Take the heads of your master's sons one by one...." Now in the first instance this might mean: "Count them, make a census, and send me the list," as though Jehu was preparing to choose a new king himself. But his letter might have another meaning. And the governors who are afraid of this general want to get in his good graces and to show him their loyalty. They thus "take the heads," i.e., cut them off. But Jehu has not actually ordered them to do this. They have interpreted his ambiguous phrase. They are not carrying out a divine order. They are taking the responsibility upon themselves, unfortunately for them.

We see here another aspect of Jehu. He is cunning. He sets traps for men, as he will do later for the worshipers of Baal. Indeed, in the story of the massacre of the priests of Baal he goes further and lies openly: "Ahab served Baal a little; but Jehu will serve him much.... I have a great sacrifice to offer Baal" (10:18f.). It is on the basis of this promise and this profession of faith that he gathers together the priests and worshipers of Baal to destroy them. Here Jehu is shown to be a liar. But then we see another aspect, looking back for a moment to the governors and ministers who have sent him the seventy heads of the sons of Ahab as a welcoming present and a means of ingratiation. Jehu has the heads exposed, then he gathers the people at Jezreel, and he begins by declaring: "Men of Israel, people, simple people, you are innocent." What has happened is not your doing. You have no hand in it. He then says that he himself is guilty: "It was I who conspired against my master and slew him." This is the greatness of Jehu, his authenticity, his strictness. He is just as strict with himself as with others. But he gives no evidence of repentance like David. With head held high, in pride, he accuses himself and recognizes that he is a traitor and assassin. But then . . . : "who struck down all these?" He is referring to the seventy heads laid out in heaps before the people. "I gave no order that this should be done. The guilty men are there—the ministers of Ahab, the governors of Ahab, the familiar friends of Ahab; these are the murderers of the sons of Ahab." At Jezreel, then, Jehu makes the innocent people into a kind of people's tribunal, and he has all these criminals of the household of Ahab executed. We thus see Jehu in the role of an accuser. Once more, he is this in the name of God. But all the same, this man who sets traps, this liar, accuser, and destroyer, has many of the attributes of Satan. We shall not pursue the matter further, but we are confronted here by the question whether all means are good if used to do the will of God (or propagate the gospel). We shall meet this question again in the final judgment of this dreadful series of events.

II

All this notwithstanding, Jehu is temporarily, before men, the earthly representative of God, of the true God. He is chosen by God and anointed king on God's behalf. He declares publicly his allegiance to Yahweh (even if without love). He has a scrupulous regard for the Word of God and the prophecies of God. He wants to obey these and fulfil them. He offers himself to the people as the man who will re-establish God's rights on earth. He abolishes false gods, idols, and idolatries. He sets up again with due

104

honor the worship of the one God and restores its purity. There can be no questioning his wish to be faithful to God at any cost. When he presents himself, it is simply as the Lord's anointed. It is from this perspective that the choices he offers are so serious. He demands decision between Baal and Yahweh. When the two messengers sent by Joram meet him and put the question: "Is it peace?" (a translation we prefer to the alternative: "Is all well?"), he replies in both instances: "What have you to do with peace? Turn round and ride behind me." He then comes to the royal palace. The queen is waiting for him. She has attired herself regally, knowing her last hour has come. She has painted herself to affirm her femininity. She has decided to die as a queen, with nobility and dignity, and as an accuser too: "You Zimri, murderer of your master." Jezebel does not tremble. She is what she has always been. She rallies herself to put a last derisory question: "Is it peace?" And again Jehu demands a choice. Turning to the servants of the queen, he poses the question: "Who is on my side?"

Three times a choice is demanded, but the "for me" really means "for Yahweh." What is important is not peace; it is to know which master to choose. And what makes the question so poignant is that the choice for God must be made contrary to all that man may hold to be good. The servants have to betray their master. A wounded man has to be handed over. A woman has to be put to death. Decision must be made for an assassin. The legitimate king of Israel has to be abandoned. Peace has to be despised. This is the choice offered by Jehu. And in fact Jehu, an incarnation of God's will at this point, claims that the choice for God must transcend all normal ethical considerations. The choice involves that "teleological suspension of the ethical" of which Kierkegaard speaks with reference to the sacrifice of Isaac by Abraham. Jehu is in fact demanding the same choice as that of Abraham. The only thing is that Jehu is not Abraham.

105

Jehu does not merely want to be a loyal servant of God. He is also endorsed by the most authentic representative of the religion of Yahweh, namely, Jehonadab the son of Rechab. Rechab, as we know, tried to re-establish in full purity the loyalty of Israel to the God of Israel. He believed this loyalty was to be found in the past, in the wilderness period, and in addition to theological orthodoxy he thus instituted an ascetic mode of life (no drinking of wine, no holding of property, a nomadic existence) in order to restore the conditions under which Israel lived in the desert, which were favorable to loyalty to the one God and which were also a witness to confidence in God. The purely spiritual sect that he founded was equally opposed both to rural conservatism with its attachment to Baal and also to urban luxury with its unchecked immorality. For we have to realize that the Baalism of Ahab and his family was not just simple idolatry. It was the "complete organization of a frenzied and orgiastic way of life." "The worship of Baal was a permanent and perpetual delirium." This is the setting of Jehonadab's reaction. Abstinence from wine signifies rejection of frenzy and debauchery. The aim is the triumph of purity in relation to the God of Israel.[1]

It is easy to criticize the ascetic attitude. But one may do this only if he is prepared to go beyond it and do better. Jehonadab, then, represents the purest belief in Yahweh, and behind the cruelty of Jehu he discerns the inflexible justiciary of divine law, a man like himself, unyielding and ascetic. He also perceives the same concern for purity and singleness of heart in God's service. He sees that in what is happening there is more than the revolt of an ambitious general. Prophecy is being fulfilled and there is a desire to worship the Lord. He is thus prepared to

[1] André Neher, *Amos: contribution à l'étude du prophetisme*; Paris: Vrin, 1950.

become Jehu's ally. And between them they bring about what might be called the religious revolution. All means are to be used to bring the people of Israel back into the right ways of the Lord, of the God who has chosen this people. This presence of Jehonadab at Jehu's side is also a guarantee of what Jehu represents at this point, God before men.

Finally and along the same lines one should not forget that God endorses Jehu's action (10:30). When the massacres are over, the Lord says to Jehu: "Because you have done well in carrying out what is right in my eyes, and have done to the house of Ahab according to all that was in my heart, your sons of the fourth generation shall sit on the throne of Israel." It is thus essential that the house of Ahab be destroyed. Jehu is commissioned to do this; it is in conformity with God's will. Elijah had announced that this would happen, and someone had to fulfil the prophecy. God does not disavow this condemnation. He does not deny that the prophecy was prophecy.

Hence Jehu alone is not responsible. He did what had to be done. Yet one must emphasize that there is a certain restraint in this expression of divine approval. We do not see the same excellent relation as that which obtains in the case of God and Elijah, or God and Abraham, or God and Moses. We do not find the same confident, paternal relation. We do not find the patience and the joy God manifests when his work is done by man. The Word of God to Jehu remains cold and distant. The level is that of a kind of necessity that God recognizes, an objective declaration, restricted approval. Your sons will reign to the fourth generation. How different are the promises to David: Your progeny will reign forever. One can hardly avoid thinking of the Mosaic commandment: "Visiting the iniquity of the fathers upon the children to the third and fourth generation of those who hate me, but showing grace to a thousand generations" (Exodus 20:5f.). And it is indeed said of

107

the successors of Jehu—Jehoahaz, Jehoash, and Jeroboam—that they did evil in the sight of the Lord, that the house of Jehu continued in the way of the sin of Jeroboam, that it was not a holy house, and that the zeal of Jehu for the Lord was quickly extinguished. It is true that among Jehu's sons there were great rulers and effective statesmen, but that is another story. Thus God grants his approval to Jehu, but with reticence. He makes promises to him, but with restrictions. This is a reminder at any rate that God does endorse the assassinations and massacres in fulfilment of the prophecy.

It would be easy enough in these circumstances to say that God is evil or that all this is in accordance with a primitive idea of God. In fact the merciless severity which God assumes ought to remind us that God says of himself that he is indeed a terrible God, a God who is slow to anger, but whose anger may be unleashed at any moment. He is the God who recognizes no limit either to his power or his demands. Even today it is still "a fearful thing to fall into the hands of the living God" (Hebrews 10:31). God is still a jealous God. That is to say, he loves to such a degree that he cannot bear it that his creature should not finally be saved. He cannot bear it that man should turn to someone other than himself. For in him alone man finds his life, his truth, his joy. Hence this jealous God cannot allow idolatry to go on indefinitely. He cannot allow crime to go unpunished indefinitely. He cannot allow man to go different ways at random. He requires that man should finally return completely to him, whatever this may cost. This will, which is the expression of the deepest love, may thus have a terrible aspect to the man who does not love God. It may seem to be dreadful and immoderate, although Abraham does not find it so. The story of Jehu constantly reminds us that when God has set his hand on a man or people, he holds them fast, and he holds them for sanctification. This man and this people must be purified.

Throughout Scripture we see that this purification is by way of testing and suffering. But the demand of God is only a sign of his supreme knowledge and wisdom. God alone knows what is truly good for man, even though man with his limited experience and truncated view is unable to see the depth of the truth and may find God's decision terrifying or tragic. This story of Jehu shows us again to what degree God sees all in one.

All the children and nephews of Ahab are viewed in Ahab himself. Individual life does not finally count. Even if one of them is good and righteous, his individual characteristics do not counterbalance his integration in Ahab. There is solidarity between them all, so that before God they are ultimately one. The Christian, however, must hear and see this in relation to Jesus Christ. Even the work of Jehu is part of God's action in Christ. To return to what we have just said, we are thus taught that God relates us all to Jesus as he related all the house of Ahab to Ahab alone, all in one. This is true both for worse (all have sinned in Adam) and also for better (all are reconciled in Christ). The affair of Ahab's house is one of many instances of this strict unity in which God holds men collectively, an exacting, terrible and unjust unity, and yet also a unity thanks to which we are saved. I might say that God manifests a unity which is tragic in detail but which is to salvation globally.

If we accept the one, however, we cannot reject the other. We must finally remember that it is the jealous God, the terrible God, the God who compliments Jehu, that Jesus has also taught us to address as Father. And we can understand this mystery only if, beginning with the revelation of God in Jesus Christ, we realize that God as Father suffers from all that his creature, his Son, suffers. He is certainly not willing, we may say, that man should be deceived, that he should go to death by separating himself from God. For he knows what is good for man. Furthermore, when he inflicts chastisement on man, God himself suffers it, for he does not withdraw from even the worst of men. God is not a judge seated apart from man and assigning blame and penalty, like a court judge, who when he has sent a convicted offender to prison goes peacefully home and takes his ease there. God is not like this. He accompanies the one he condemns both to prison and to hell. He leaves his peaceful heaven and takes upon himself all that man undergoes. Ahab has not just let loose the wrath of God; he has made God suffer. Ahab has made God suffer not only because he persecuted the servants of the Lord but because Ahab himself was condemned and rejected by God. God took upon himself what he inflicted on Ahab, just as he took upon himself and suffered the massacre of Ahab's house according to his own judgment. When Jehu fulfilled the prophecy, it was on God himself that his violence fell. It was God whom he massacred in the priests of Baal, none of whom was a stranger or unimportant to God, since the Father had numbered all the hairs of their heads too. All the violence of Jehu is assumed by Jesus Christ. Nor was it just the executioners, enemies of God, and idolaters who crucified God in Jesus Christ; it was also the champions of Yahweh, the knights, the crusaders, Elijah slaying the priests of Baal and Jehu extirpating the house of Ahab. It is in this way and in these conditions that Jehu does the will of God. In his zeal for God, it is God himself he strikes. But it had to be thus; this was inevitable. It is only in this way and in these conditions that God's will was the destruction of the house of Ahab. It is God's will only to the degree that he takes upon himself the chastisement that he wills and ordains, the chastisement of man, his suffering and his death.[2]

2 All this has been said already, and far better than here, by W. Vischer, *The Witness to Christ in the Old Testament,* Vol. I.

III

But the story of Jehu does not stop here. Once he has seized power and accomplished his mission of extirpation, Jehu does not have a glorious reign. Threatened by Hazael and by Assyria, he turns to the latter in self-protection. He becomes the vassal of Shalmaneser III, pays him tribute, and a relief shows him on his knees before the Assyrian king. But Hazael succeeds in repelling the Assyrians and pays Jehu back for the alliance. The king of Israel is regularly defeated "throughout the territory of Israel" (2 Kings 10:32). This certainly does not accord very well with the glory and the power of being the faithful champion of God. The latter is no assurance of victory. Another point worth noting is that during the twenty-eight years of his reign Elisha does not seem to have stepped forth a single time to help and deliver Israel. The fact is that Jehu is no ally of the prophets. He scorns them. He doubts their political competence. He has no time for the prophecy of Elijah which set Elisha over him. He also aims at the throne of Judah after slaying the king of Judah. But he knows that in Judah he will come up against the opposition of the priests and Levites who cannot accept any king except a descendant of David. He is also aware that the prophets will not help him in this venture. This is why he sets them aside and makes his own decisions without consulting anyone. Elisha remains silent.[3] Not until the reign of his grandson Joash, as we have seen, does the dying Elisha announce Israel's victories. But this is not the problem. A century later, in the time of the third descendant of Jehu, the prophet Hosea proclaims the condemnation of Jehu and his family. When Hosea has a son by the harlot, the Lord says: "Call his name Jezreel; for yet a little while, and I will punish the house of Jehu

[3] Neher, *op. cit.*, pp. 182f.

for the blood of Jezreel, and I will put an end to the kingdom of the house of Israel. And on that day I will break the bow of Israel in the valley of Jezreel" (Hosea 1:4-5).

Here, then, we have the implacable nexus of violence and ensuing violence. Jehu has taken the sword. He has shed blood at Jezreel as Ahab did at Jezreel. Hence in their turn the descendants of Jehu will be punished and destroyed at Jezreel. But why? Does Jehu have to be punished like Ahab, but this time for having fulfilled the prophecy, for having been faithful to God, for having been a zealot, for having re-established the worship of the true God? Having been praised by God, is he now to be punished for the very thing on account of which he was praised? Surely a massacre is not enough to explain the punishment, for David, too, was a destroyer. And what about Elisha? What is the reason, then, for this unlikely decision of God? The text indicates that Jehu fell into the error of Jeroboam, that he did not turn aside from the sins of Jeroboam, that he did not keep the law of the Lord with all his heart. The sin of Jeroboam, which plays such an important part throughout this political history, will be studied in the next chapter, and we shall see that it will confirm the interpretation we shall now attempt.

The real question in the case of Jehu is that of the heart. Like Abraham, one may say, Jehu is set outside the morality which God established. But Jehu is not Abraham. In fact Jehu is a man who, faithful to God and knowing his will, commandeers this will and makes it his own. He identifies his own cause with God's design. He thus sets out to shape history in the name of God but also in the place of God. No doubt he does everything exactly as prophesied. No doubt he achieves what the Lord intends. But it is now his own affair. He has substituted his own will for God's. It is he who does it; he does not let the Lord act through him. He puts a screen between history and the Lord of history. For man can always erect this barrier and achieve his own purpose. What was God's purpose has become purely and simply the autonomous will of Jehu. He seizes control of the prophecy. He makes it his own cause, confident that he is in the line of God's will. He himself has decided to fulfil the prophecy. We are in the presence here of religious voluntarism. When he has killed Joram, he orders the officer to throw his body in the field of Jezreel because it is necessary that the prophecy be intentionally and literally fulfilled. Similarly, when he decides to put the ministers and governors to death, he declares: "Know then that there shall fall to the earth nothing of the word of the Lord, which the Lord spoke concerning the house of Ahab." This is an admirable declaration of scrupulous fidelity. But what it is really saying is that I, Jehu, will apply in all strictness what has been a Word of the Lord.

Wanting to put into effect God's decision, he pays no attention to the great statement that it is not of him that wills nor of him that runs. Jehu is one of those in the Bible who want to fulfil and accomplish of themselves what God has said. Thus Abraham wants to fulfil the promise of posterity by his own decision and at his own time, i.e., by means of Hagar. This is the whole problem. Will the Word of God seize us? Will we subject our own will to God's? Even Jesus is tempted in this respect: "If you are the Son of God. . . ." Will Jesus yield and prove in his own way that he is the Son of God? Will he, independently of the Father, decide that he is the Son of God? Will he perform the miracle that Satan asks for at the beginning of his ministry? Will he perform the miracle that the crowd wants from him on the cross? Will he regard the title Son of God as a prey to be snatched after? In fact, if he had performed the miracle of jumping from the temple or coming down from the cross he would have been the master of the Word of God. He would have chosen his own way. The same applies in the further temptation: I will give you all the kingdoms of the world. He knows that his Father has made him Lord of all the kingdoms of the world. Thus if he accedes to the devil's request he will be fulfilling precisely the intention of God, but he will be doing it by his own means, at his own time, and according to his own decision. This is the temptation. One must wait for the hour that God has chosen. One must accept God's means. Abraham must wait until Sarah becomes a mother.

This will show that Abraham's own initiative, although successful (for Ishmael is born), is definitely abortive and sterile. We are thus put in a cruel dilemma. God makes his will known to us. We must will it and do it ourselves. We must decide on our own to do it. This is unquestionable. Nevertheless, we must not take over God's Word. We must not substitute our own intention, time, or means for those of God, which alone are good and right. This is where Jehu goes astray. He does not let himself be seized by God's Word; he seizes it. Perhaps there is a hint of this already in the name of his birthplace. Jehu comes from Ramoth, which means "precious and exalted things that are difficult to grasp." But the root means "to exalt oneself," "to be proud." This also sheds light on another aspect of the alliance with Jehonadab. For Rechab, too, is an example of spiritual voluntarism. He wants to recover through asceticism the moral purity and fidelity of ancient Israel. The inspiration of this fidelity does not proceed, then, from the heart. It proceeds from a set of practices and conditions which are accepted in order to attest, to bear witness to this fidelity. In the sphere of law and religion Jehonadab acts as Jehu does in the sphere of prophecy and politics. But if Jehu is sure of doing the will of God, if, having heard the Word of God, he wants to do it in its entirety, if he believes he has been commissioned by God to turn what has been written into a historical event, then all means employed are good. Once he sets out to achieve God's objective, the instruments do not matter much.

In other words, Jehu becomes a politician like all the rest, using all the weapons of politics. His extreme opposition to Baalism is probably due to political calculation: "If the reign of Jehu is not to be ephemeral, if a new dynasty is to be installed on the throne of Samaria, it is necessary that this reign be inaugurated in a completely new way."[4] Jehu was acquainted with the *coup d'état* of Zimri. Zimri assassinated the king and reigned for twelve years. To found a dynasty it was necessary that the kingdom be founded on principles and an ideal. An extreme anti-Baalism had to be substituted for the extreme Baalism of the sons of Ahab. This becomes a principle of government. Officially everything reminiscent of Baalism is suppressed. But soon Baalism reappears. One may thus conclude that Jehu's action was purely external. His authoritarian anti-Baalism was not based on spiritual power, on obedience of the heart to the Lord. It thus becomes hypocrisy. It is a "fiction for reasons of state."[5] Jehu uses prophecy in the interests of politics while pretending to use politics in the service of prophecy. He wants to do what God has revealed but he confuses what God has shown will come to pass with what God really loves. The same confusion is shown by those who want to pluck out the tares from the field, or by the disciples when they want to call down fire from heaven on unrepentant villages, or by Judas when he too does what God has said will come to pass. But Jehu has also taken over the good. He does not leave control in God's hands. He pretends to be practicing a politics taken from Holy Scripture. Now that God has spoken, Jehu thinks he has abdicated in favor of man. God is no longer the living God who decides and conducts. He is the God of yesterday who has announced the condemnation of Ahab. Today the condemnation of Ahab is up to Jehu. He does not have to consult God. He has simply to follow the Word

4 *Ibid.*, pp. 184f.
5 *Loc. cit.*

115

which was spoken yesterday and which is no longer a living Word. For Jehu, God has no today. He has only a kind of fixed permanence. In other words, he is not the living God. We must be very careful in this regard. For the temptation to treat God thus is not merely the temptation of those who practice a politics taken from Holy Scripture, or an ethics of the same type, against whom it is easy to be on guard. It is also the temptation of those who speak of the incompleteness of creation and of the task of man to complete and develop it by his own means. It is the temptation of those who speak of the "demiurgic" function of man. Jehu is the prototype of demiurgic politics. The whole question may in fact be reduced to two points—the inner attitude, and the choice of means.

We are always tempted to think that all means are good once they are subjected to the will of God (inwardly) or oriented to the end that God seeks. We fail to see that this always amounts to the fallacy that "the end justifies the means," and we justify ourselves hypocritically by invoking the dictum that "to the pure all things are pure." In fact, as these stories have progressively shown, the choice of means is our great responsibility. All means are not good in doing God's work. Now at this point we all insist strongly today on the difference between proselytism and evangelism. No one will tolerate the inquisition or dragooning any longer. Yet we are only too ready to permit the use of mass media, of television, in the propagation of the gospel. We think that the technical methods of the world are ultimately legitimate. And when we choose political means, it is by moral, cultural, and humanist criteria that we make the choice (e.g., democracy, elections, etc.). Now in this context we cannot explore the problem of means with any completeness.[6] But we must

---

6 We have studied it already in *The Presence of the Kingdom*, and we shall consider it from another angle in *Ethics*, Vol. II.

remember its crucial importance. If from another standpoint we adopt a popular term in modern theology, that of transparency, we might say that Jehu is the opaque man. In Jesus there is full transparency between God and man; we see the fulness of God in him. Nothing interposes between the two. The same is true to some degree of John the Baptist, although he does not attain the fulness of self-divestation which Jesus alone could attain because he was the Son of God. As John says of himself: "He must increase, but I must decrease" (John 3:30). Jehu, however, is a man who interposes himself while pretending to be accomplishing the purpose of God. He does not allow us to see the work of God and the love of the Lord through these terrible and tragic actions. This is why Elisha is silent during his reign. The Word of God is no longer spoken. Jehu's revolution is not really religious. It makes the presence of the Lord more incomprehensible to men. For in it man is finally the master of his own life. He alone conducts it. He does not divest himself. He does not renounce himself. He is just and has no remorse. He does not see what he has to repent of. For he has done all to the greater glory of God and in the affirmation of his power.

Now if there is this opacity in Jehu, it is not just because of his inner attitude, his affirmation that "I alone have done it." It is also because of his choice of the means of action; these are the means of the average politician, the kind of means that Machiavelli would not hesitate to recommend. Jehu has decided to make the people faithful to God. He uses political means to force the people into this faithfulness, this worship, this religion. We must always be aware of the important truth that our means are the thing which creates opacity between God and men, far more so than our person. What constitutes the veil, the misunderstanding, is what we choose as the instrument of action, of mediation, of intervention, of influence.

For it is by this that men finally judge. This is what men

see, resent, understand, and experience; nothing else, and certainly not our intentions. By his actual choice of means, Jehu is not a witness to the God who shows mercy to a thousand generations, but rather to the God who exterminates and chastises without pity. By his actual choice of means he has separated in men's eyes and for men the two faces of God, the two hands of God. For this reason, he himself will have to have dealings with a God who shows mercy only to three generations. For he is a type of the man who is unfaithful even in his faithfulness. He is both approved by God and also rejected by him. To be sure, he is always loved by God in spite of his lies, assassinations, and treacheries. But he is also rejected by God because of his commandeering of the Word and the harshness of his loyalty. The real tragedy, however, is that he is finally the reason for the rejection of the whole people, and the reference is very plainly to him in the extraordinary saying which Hosea speaks to Israel: "I have given you kings (a king) in my anger, and I have taken them away (will take him away) in my wrath" (Hosea 13:11). The best possible king could only provoke the anger of the Lord after having been the agent of his wrath.

After this experience it seems as though there is in fact nothing more to hope for in the Northern Kingdom.

Even when the king is faithful and leads the people to God, everything is still false and ambiguous. Thus God makes the big decision. The four descendants of Jehu will reign, and then there will only be troubled reigns, periods of injustice and evil, full of revolutions and defeats, until the great collapse of Israel, the capture and destruction of Samaria, and the deportation of the people to Assyrian captivity.

This is the story and drama of Jehu, whose very name may perhaps mean: "Is it possible that he exists?"

V

Ahaz

2 Kings 16:1-20

1 In the seventeenth year of Pekah the son of Remaliah, Ahaz the son of Jotham, king of Judah, began to reign. 2 Ahaz was twenty years old when he began to reign, and he reigned sixteen years in Jerusalem. And he did not do what was right in the eyes of the Lord his God, as his father David had done, 3 but he walked in the way of the kings of Israel. He even burned his son as an offering, according to the abominable practices of the nations whom the Lord drove out before the people of Israel. 4 And he sacrificed and burned incense on the high places, and on the hills, and under every green tree.

5 Then Rezin king of Syria and Pekah the son of Remaliah, king of Israel, came up to wage war on Jerusalem, and they besieged Ahaz but could not conquer him. 6 At that time the king of Edom recovered Elath for Edom, and drove the men of Judah from Elath; and the Edomites came to Elath, where they dwell to this day. 7 So Ahaz sent messengers to Tiglath-pileser king of Assyria, saying, "I am your servant and your son. Come up, and rescue me from the hand of the king of Syria and from the hand of the king of Israel, who are attacking me." 8 Ahaz also took the silver and gold that was found in the house of the Lord and in the treasures of the king's house, and sent a present to the king of Assyria. 9 And the king of Assyria hearkened to him; the king of Assyria marched up against Damascus, and took it, carrying its people captive to Kir, and he killed Rezin.

10 When King Ahaz went to Damascus to meet Tiglath-pileser king of Assyria, he saw the altar that was at Damascus. And King Ahaz sent to Uriah the priest a model of the altar, and its pattern, exact in all its details. 11 And Uriah the priest built the altar; in accordance with all that King Ahaz had sent from Damascus, so

Uriah the priest made it, before King Ahaz arrived from Damascus. 12 And when the king came from Damascus, the king viewed the altar. Then the king drew near to the altar, and went up on it, 13 and burned his burnt offering and his cereal offering, and poured his drink offering, and threw the blood of his peace offerings upon the altar. 14 And the bronze altar which was before the Lord he removed from the front of the house, from the place between his altar and the house of the Lord, and put it on the north side of his altar. 15 And King Ahaz commanded Uriah the priest, saying, "Upon the great altar burn the morning burnt offering, and the evening cereal offering, and the king's burnt offering, and his cereal offering, with the burnt offering of all the people of the land, and their cereal offering, and their drink offering; and throw upon it all the blood of the burnt offering, and all the blood of the sacrifice; but the bronze altar shall be for me to inquire by." 16 Uriah the priest did all this, as King Ahaz commanded.

17 And King Ahaz cut off the frames of the stands, and removed the laver from them, and he took down the sea from off the bronze oxen that were under it, and put it upon a pediment of stone. 18 And the covered way for the sabbath which had been built inside the palace, and the outer entrance for the king he removed from the house of the Lord, because of the kings of Assyria. 19 Now the rest of the acts of Ahaz which he did, are they not written in the Book of the Chronicles of the Kings of Judah? 20 And Ahaz slept with his fathers, and was buried with his fathers in the city of David; and Hezekiah his son reigned in his stand.

Elisha is dead. We pass now to the kingdom of Judah and we find Ahaz, whom we might describe as the exact opposite of Jehu. We have said that everything Jehu did stood under the sign of ambiguity. Unfaithful even in his faithfulness, fulfilling God's design but putting himself in God's place, legalizing prophecy, Jehu is a man whose words are also those of duplicity. In contrast, Ahaz is a man whose choice is single. There is no ambiguity or difficulty about him. He has no concern for God at all. There is thus no tension, conflict, or confusion. He is all of a piece, but on the bad side. He has chosen idolatry in all its forms. His vocation is exclusively political. And during the sixteen years of his reign in Jerusalem, the prophetic word of Isaiah, confronted by the silence of the king, falls in the void and seems to be useless.

Compared with what has gone before, the situation is a new and surprising one. Ahaz and Isaiah are two men who practically never meet. We shall see later that when God wants to send help to Ahaz, the latter ignores the promise and goes his own way. The king obviously does not believe when God orders him through Isaiah: "Ask a sign of the Lord your God." He does not want to ask anything from God, to receive anything from him, to owe anything to him. And he finds an ironical pretext for refusing: "I will not put the Lord to the test." In fact he is convinced that God is nothing and can do nothing (Isaiah 7:10-12). This refusal of Ahaz is a mark of his whole reign.

I

A first and important aspect of Ahaz is set before us in the statement: "He walked in the way of the kings of Israel. He even burned his son as an offering [he probably offered up his firstborn son in sacrifice]." Now this statement is obviously referring to what the previous chapters call the sin of Jeroboam, since this characterizes the ways of the kings of Israel. Omri, Ahab, Joram, Jehu and all his sons committed the sin of Jeroboam. We must now try to see what this implies, since it is of great importance in the case of Ahaz, king of Judah. If we turn to the story of Jeroboam (1 Kings 12), we see that this leader of the people rises up against the lawful king, Rehoboam, the son of Solomon. He organizes a kind of *coup d'état.* But he is expressly obeying what the prophet Ahijah told him. In this famous scene the prophet tore his mantle and gave ten parts to Jeroboam representing the gift from God of ten of the tribes of Israel. Thus Jeroboam was chosen by God to achieve his own purpose. But there is always an "if". . . . "If you will hearken to all that I command you, and will walk in my ways, and do what is right in my eyes . . . " (1 Kings 11:38). This is what Yahweh says. Jeroboam, then, breaks with the lawful kings and founds the kingdom of Israel. But then he makes two bulls of gold and says to the people: "Behold your gods, O Israel, who brought you up out of the land of Israel" (2 Kings 12:38). Now this has given rise to a misunderstanding. Many commentators have thought that the king set up an idolatrous cult at Bethel and Dan, a cult of false gods. The sin of Jeroboam against the Lord is that he leads Israel into worship of the bull. But this does not seem to be the real point.

Too much stress has been laid on the story of the bulls. Specialists agree that these were not images of the deity or of other gods than Yahweh, but rather a footstool for the invisible deity. They were not idols of Yahweh but an attribute. Essentially the problem is no more than that of the choice of Jerusalem as the only cultic site. This Deuteronomic idea, however, simply cloaks a more profound reality. For the celebrated cult at Bethel and Dan is in fact the cult of Yahweh.

The cult of Yahweh is maintained but with a visible representation. Jeroboam remains faithful to the one Lord, but he gives him a face. There is, then, no theological or liturgical change. Israel is in the right way. This is confirmed by the distinction often made between false gods and the sin of Jeroboam (which also yielded in time to other cults). Thus Joram overthrows the altars of Baal, Ishtar, and the gods introduced by Ahab, but he retains the way of Jeroboam. Jehu himself, as we have seen, restores everywhere the worship of the true God, but he also commits again the sin of Jeroboam. This is also confirmed, as we shall see later, by Ahaz himself, who proceeds to do at Jerusalem what Jeroboam did in Samaria, although without setting up statues of bulls. What was, then, the sin of Jeroboam?

One is naturally reminded of the permanent idolatry

which drives Israel to fertility gods, to the bull as the force of reproduction. This was already a temptation in the wilderness. But the sin of Jeroboam is more precise. Two complementary elements should be kept in mind. He made graven images of creatures to represent God, thus transgressing the second commandment. He then led the people to worship elsewhere than in the temple at Jerusalem and to offer sacrifices elsewhere than on the great altar of Solomon. But this still does not seem very convincing to us. Some would question whether the two precepts at issue even existed in the days of Jeroboam. In any case, the actual concentration of worship in the one temple, and possibly the law as we now know it, might well have belonged to a later period.

More important and decisive is the fact that Jeroboam set up priests who were not Levites (for perhaps these seemed to be too revolutionary for him) but were simply mediators of any type. Now this denotes rejection of the symbol which God selected to remind Israel incessantly of his intervention and election by pure grace. This is undoubtedly true.[1] Yet even this does not exhaust the significance of the sin of Jeroboam.

For if Jeroboam's reform results in the canonization of the cultus, it is also, as finely shown by Neher, a reaction against the cultural influence of Phoenicia. In choosing high places like Bethel and Dan, the king is protesting against Phoenician customs which were becoming widespread in Israel. He aims to restore the patriarchal customs of Israel. This is also the motive which leads Jehu to maintain the two shrines. Thus the actuality of Jeroboam's sin is very complex, for there is intermingled in it an authentic fidelity. And this enables us to justify what might seem to be paradoxical, namely, a discussion of the sin of Jeroboam in relation to Ahaz, who has nothing

[1] On the sin of Jeroboam cf. especially Vischer, *Les premiers prophètes*, p. 391; Neher, *Amos*, p. 190; von Rad, *Theology*, I, 58.

whatever to do with the sanctuaries of Bethel and Dan, who celebrated the cultus at Jerusalem, and who did not have a statue of the bull set up. Nevertheless, it seems to us that he is rightly said to have followed the errors of the kings of Israel, errors that are always summed up in the sin of Jeroboam. Furthermore, it does not seem that the actuality of this sin is tied to a given representation or place. On the contrary, the text shows what is meant: Jeroboam said in his heart, "Now the kingdom will turn back to the house of David; if this people go up to offer sacrifices in the house of the Lord at Jerusalem, then the heart of this people will turn again to their lord, to Rehoboam king of Judah . . . " (1 Kings 12:26-27). This is the reason why Jeroboam makes the golden calves and orders that the people should not go to Jerusalem to worship Yahweh but worship him instead at Bethel and Dan. This is even more remarkable if one grants, as is quite possible, that the two calves were situated in frontier towns to the north and south of the kingdom. Yahweh was apparently instituted the political guardian of the borders of Israel. Jeroboam's aim was to keep the people at home, to stop them from crossing the frontiers, to avoid all contacts with the enemy. He thought that if Israel continued to make constant journeys to Jerusalem it would succumb to the prestige of the capital, regret the division, and want to return to Rehoboam. The aim, then, was to maintain the separation of God's people, to safeguard the independence of the new nation. The men of Israel must not go to Jerusalem. There must be a new capital of Israel with all the attributes of a capital. There must be a God of Israel worshiped in Israel, for at this period the national and perhaps the territorial character of God was still the current sentiment. If the people of Israel was to remain an independent national entity, it had to believe that its God, Yahweh, was not attached to the territory of the two tribes but had his dwelling in Israel too. In other words, the sin of Jeroboam was precisely that he made theological and religious decisions regarding the true God for political reasons, thus subordinating the spiritual life of the people to political necessity, orienting its worship, not to another lord, but according to the demands of politics, seizing control of the revelation of God, playing the role of the prophet in order to distinguish the true God. "Behold your gods . . . who brought you up out of the land of Egypt" (1 Kings 12:28). It is thus the state which sets its seal on both the truth of revelation and also the conditions in which the people will hear and worship. But when the state does this, it is for political motives. What we have here, then, is not an idolatrous state but a political power which creates a state religion or which uses the truth of God, the revelation of God, and the work of God for political ends. It subordinates the will of God, not to its own will, but to the greater good of the nation or the state. It integrates God's work into the imperative of a realistic policy.

The great aim of Jeroboam was the security of the kingdom of Israel. To achieve this he took the necessary material steps. He built cities and forts, Shechem and Penuel.[2] But he also took spiritual and psychological steps. We see here the intentional and deliberate establishment of a national religion in the service of the state and for the purpose of unifying national sentiment. There is nothing at all "primitive" about this. It is just what we do too. Every modern state thinks that it should establish in the same way a full-scale religion which will serve to unite the people and make it loyal to the political power, integrating the church so that it will be "national" and will fill this same role.

The sin of Jeroboam, which is repeated by all the kings of Israel and by Ahaz, is not the result of a primitive view of the deity. It is rather the result of an enduring political

[2] For a discussion of this work, see my study of the city in the Bible (*The Meaning of the City*; Grand Rapids: Eerdmans, 1970).

125

necessity. A state is insecure unless there is a state religion. Politics demands religion as an ally. But Jeroboam's problem is that the pure revelation of Yahweh cannot be integrated into politics. It cannot be exploited in this way because it is the fact of the living God. Hence the revelation has to be transformed into a religion that can be exploited. The Lord of heaven and earth, whom no man can see without perishing, has to be transformed into a golden bull. Certainly it is still God who is worshiped. But he is worshiped in the form of a bull. And the striking thing is that the nations round about also worship bulls. To be sure, what is signified is not the same. But what signifies is. Bulls are a sign of fertility, of reproductive force, of wealth, of happiness. But is not this true of Yahweh too? Cannot the two be combined? May not the symbols of the nations be used to represent the God of Israel, since the symbolism is the same? If so, two things are achieved at a single stroke. Loyalty is maintained to the God of Israel, and reassurance is given to the people, which is constantly looking aside to the efficacious gods of others. Once again we are directly concerned here. Our golden calves are money, the economy, communism, capitalism, science, history, the state. All these are supposed to grant us happiness in virtue of their abundant creative force. These calves, too, are in the hands of the state, which uses them as a religious power to promote ultimately its own grandeur and the effectiveness of its policies. This is the sin of Jeroboam which Ahaz introduces into Judah.

II

At a first glance Ahaz does not seem to have the same motives, since he is not trying to prevent contacts between Israel and Judah. But this was only a casual motive, as we have seen. The deeper aim remains. At issue is the power of the state, and the use of religion to achieve it. Ahaz is in serious straits. He is attacked by a coalition of Damascus and the kingdom of Israel. These want to set up in Jerusalem a monarchy of the Canaanite type. Ahaz must defend both his monarchy and his state. When the coalition is known, God, who always takes the initiative, addresses Ahaz through his prophet Isaiah (Isaiah 7:1-9). His message is: "Do not be afraid; do not let your heart be troubled; you will not be defeated; only believe." God is in truth the Savior of Israel, and the prophecy is to the effect that if you do not believe you will perish. This is God's appeal to his people and its king. It is both a summons and also a threat, and yet it is first of all a promise, a guarantee that "it shall not come to pass" (7:7).

Ahaz, already a rebellious king, is in the great patience of God called to faith yet again. But Ahaz is panic-stricken. "His heart . . . shook as the trees of the forest shake before the wind" (7:2). Furthermore, he does not want to listen. He has already reached his decision. There is for him no question of turning to the protector of Israel, to the Lord. In his eyes God is no longer the master of the nations, the one who holds in his hands the destiny of his own and every people. The only place for God is in a political combination as the object of the national religion.

The sensible thing to do according to Ahaz was to appeal to the greatest power in the Orient, Assyria. But some arrangement had to be reached with the Assyrians. Money and gifts might help (v. 8), but these were not enough. In the Orient Israel's claim to be the people of God was well known, as was also its claim that Yahweh could not be compared to any other. The religious exclusivism of this God was common knowledge. This provided the ground for accommodation. Ahaz went to see the king of Assyria. There he made an accurate model, an "image" (the very word Genesis uses when it says that God made man in his own image), of the altar which Tiglath-pileser had had set up in Damascus after capturing the city, and he ordered that an exact replica of this altar should be set up in the temple at Jerusalem. Now this altar was in reality an altar of the god Hadad.

Uriah the priest did as he was told, and then the king celebrated the praises of the Lord on the idolatrous altar (which was undoubtedly adorned with calves). He offered there the burnt offering, the libations and the peace offering. He instructed the priest that from now on all sacrifices should be offered on this altar. Then "in honor of the king of Assyria" (v. 18) he changed "the covered way for the sabbath and the outer entrance for the king." His aim was to please the king of Assyria, to gain his friendship, to assure him of the loyalty of the king of Judah. This is why he brought in all these Assyrian symbols. What clearer pledge could there be than the adoption of the religion of this powerful ally? What he did is just the same as what was done by those who, seeking the support of Hitler, adopted the Nazi doctrine of the state and anti- Semitism. It is what is being done by those who, relying on the U.S.S.R., espouse the cause of communism. Ahaz's objective is the same as that of Jeroboam but with a slant to foreign policy rather than domestic policy as in the case of the king of Israel. There is the same exploiting of a god who is useful to the state, who can be an instrument of policy, who is like the gods of men so far as his significance is concerned. Ahaz does not even seem to have had the same problems of conscience as Jeroboam. The latter wanted to remain faithful to Yahweh. His attitude was as follows: "Fundamentally, in the worship of the heart, in the authenticity of faith, we are looking to Yahweh even though it be under the form of a bull, for obviously our attachment is not to the sign as such." Ahaz has no such scruples. He just fashions a religion that will please the Assyrians. He adopts the sign without worrying about what is signified. He sets up a god like that of the nations, identifying Yahweh with the Assyrian god. What matters is the sign which is given, the setting up of a replica of the Assyrian altar. And to mark the break many acts are performed indicating the evacuation of God. The treasures dedicated to the Lord, the precious things and temple utensils, are given to the king of Assyria. Then Ahaz destroys the great altar set up by Solomon. He cuts off the frames of the stands, takes away the ornaments, and removes the altar to a distant place (vv. 14, 17). He pulls down the sea from off the bronze oxen, the basin of purification, and puts it on a pediment of stone, probably to one side. One point especially should be noted: "The bronze altar which was before the face of the Lord he removed from the front of the house" (v. 14). Now this undoubtedly means that the altar in question was up in the front of the temple, but one can perhaps catch a spiritual sense too. This was the altar which God had chosen to be in his presence, and when the king removed it he was removing God's own presence. This altar was not to be in the Lord's presence. Yet appearances had to be kept up, for the people of Judah clung to its God, the God who had been revealed to it and who had chosen it. Just as Jeroboam claimed: "Behold your gods . . . who brought you up out of the land of Israel," because it was the true God he wanted to worship, so Ahaz keeps up appearances, observing all the ordinances laid down by Yahweh. He retains the priests, not setting up a new clergy. He also retains the rites, the sacrifices, the burnt offerings, the morning and evening offerings. So far as the people of Judah can see, nothing has changed. Only the form of the altar has been altered.

Now we are always prone to say: "What matters is faith. What matters is the contribution of true faith to these rites and offerings. The rest is empty form. . . ." In reality, however, this is just an easy way out; it is self-justification. The altar which Ahaz destroyed was decreed by God no less than revelation. The temple had been built according to the order and model given by God. It is not a matter of trying to find out whether this was a true revelation or command or was only presented as such, for two factors have to be taken into account. First, the directions are given in Holy Scripture, and we have to take this seriously even if we do not take it absolutely literally. Then in the days of Ahaz it was commonly believed that the directions were direct revelations of God, and what counts is the intention of Ahaz in relation to this belief. His attitude is the same as that of Jeroboam. The God of Abraham, Isaac, and Jacob will be retained, but his orders and ordinances will be ignored and altered. He will be worshiped and served in another way. In reality, however, he will be made to serve our way. There is in fact an altering of the revealed God himself, for the revealed God gives himself to us in a specific form. Nor are we at liberty to change this form in relation to God, for God himself has selected the form. It is a constant temptation to think, in the interests of utility or convenience, that the form God has taken in self-revelation is of no importance. But when we take liberties with the form, we are really taking liberties with God himself. Ahaz changes the revelation when he changes the signs of the revealed God. By changing the order that God has set up, he renounces God himself. He transforms the living God into an idol, the wind of the Spirit (who chose to reside in the temple of Solomon) into a utilitarian religion. For Ahaz the really decisive thing is what is of value to maintain the independence of the people of Judah, to save it from destruction at the hands of the invaders from the north. Some concessions may surely be made to this end. Again, we have here an enduring problem. The nation has to be saved, and so some of its values may be abandoned, for if they are not, the nation itself will go down and then everything will be lost. *Primum vivere!* Dirty hands! This is not just a modern question. In fact, however, a Judah which denies its God no longer has any reason to exist at all. Imitating the Assyrian, Judah might just as well die. Its truth has perished before its life.

Ahaz, then, is swayed by what will help to save the people. He fashions a religion similar to that of his allies. He does this for political reasons, and his political calculations finally prove to be right. The king of Assyria agrees to come to the aid of this loyal ally. He captures Damascus, leads its people off into captivity, and puts its king to death. But in face of this Assyrian victory and the success of Ahaz, it is all the more impressive to recall the prophecy which Isaiah is issuing at this very moment against the Assyrian (Isaiah 10:5-19). At the very summit of his glory, the Assyrian is marked out for destruction. And the unheard of thing is that Ahaz is the occasion of this judgment. The Assyrian has become the persecutor of Israel at the request of Ahaz, and God will take up the cause of Israel.

In a fairly short space of time the Assyrian is condemned to vanish. A further point to be noted here is that at this juncture Isaiah seems to be playing the part of a traitor to his own people. He speaks for the enemy, attacking his people's allies. He does so at the very moment of his people's victory, of its deliverance, of an incontestable political success.[3]

Furthermore, the war against Judah heralds the imminent end of the Northern Kingdom and the captivity. Ahaz enjoyed a political success, but what was there now in common between the ten tribes of the North and the two of the South. How could they be any longer the twelve tribes of the chosen people? And what had brought about

[3] The date of the prophecy is obviously open to discussion. All the victories to which the text refers are between 738 and 722 B.C. (during the reign of Ahaz) apart from that of Carchemish in 717 B.C. This was after Ahaz and it has led some to argue that the prophecy was later too; if so, what is written above does not really belong to this context, but the main point is not affected.

this unpardonable war, the unleashing of the Assyrian by Ahaz, which would finally bring about the deportation of the people? The answer is Jeroboam's sin, which had been to put politics first and to maintain the independence of the new nation, and the sin of Ahaz, which was also to put politics first and to use political means, without consulting God's intention, to save the Southern Kingdom, Jerusalem, the temple and the symbol of God. Thus the kings pursue their politics without bothering about God's will. Their politics, however, can only imply conformity to the world, to the world of nations, and they carry this conformity even to the point of trying to bring Yahweh into the political game. What led to this unpardonable war was putting politics first, obsession with politics, the pursuit of politics above all else. Now Ahaz, like Ahab, was a good politician. He was successful. And we may note once again how free from prejudice the authors of the stories are. They are not afraid to show how strong and victorious the enemies of God were. Irrespective of the spiritual price which had to be paid, the price in truth and the price in love, Ahaz conformed the revelation of God to the world, and he was successful. He sought above all things efficiency at the human level, and he was successful. This reminds us again of Jehu. He, too, wanted to succeed. But he did so in order to accomplish God's will. In effect we have seen that his concern to be effective led him to complete betrayal. He, too, committed the sin of Jeroboam. He, too, put political action first. We thus have two contrasting examples, a king who is concerned about God's will and wants to keep step with God, and a king who has no regard at all for the Lord. Yet in spite of the great difference, these two kings are on the same plane. If they had met they would have hated one another. Nevertheless, they are alike in their concern for success and their readiness to put politics first, even though the one believed in

God and the other did not. Their likeness was certainly not a happy one.

It was in these circumstances that Isaiah made his extraordinary prophecy (7-8). The prophet carried God's promise to the king and offered to back it by a miracle. The king, however, refused this. Then Isaiah accused and challenged Ahaz. The king had tried God's patience, and because of him all the house of David would be punished. Ahaz himself was rejected as king. But man's unfaithfulness cannot shake God's faithfulness. Hence the prophet declares: "Therefore the Lord himself will give you a sign. Behold, a young woman shall conceive and bear a son, and shall call his name Immanuel" (7:14). God with us. God will keep his promise in its entirety. Then in a strange passage Isaiah speaks of a "conspiracy" of God (8:11-15). The point is that even though Ahaz is still alive God has proclaimed another king on the throne of David, who eliminates descent from David according to the flesh, and substitutes the true son of David, Wonderful Counselor, he who is to come, but who is already announced in the time of Isaiah, present with Isaiah himself and the children Yahweh gave him.[4] The political sagacity of Ahaz, then, is too great. It gets in the way of the fulfilment of God's gracious purpose to establish the universal and saving kingdom of Immanuel, God with us.

III

All this leads us to consider in this context the problem of efficacy. It is at once very true and yet over-facile to say that the Holy Spirit alone is efficacious. The Holy Spirit is efficacious in the realm of creation, both the original creation and the new creation at the end of the age. He is

---

[4] On all this cf. the admirable analysis of W. Vischer, "La prophétie d'Emmanuel et la fête royale de Sion," *Études théologiques et religieuses*, 1954.

also efficacious in individual life and in history, where he creates facts and situations and initiates chains of actions. He is efficacious in the sphere of redemption; it is he who makes the work of Jesus Christ actual and living for the individual. He is efficacious in giving effect to what men do when they are oriented to God and try to express revelation. He activates our prayers and preaching and works. In all this there is no intrinsic logic, no closed system, no automatic action. The effect of our acts in these areas springs from God's free decision but it is not independent of our own will and work. God does not act arbitrarily. He does not act alone in human history or intervene *ex nihilo*. God makes his will known to us. It is in doing this will of God that we may enjoy the intervention of the Holy Spirit as the presence of the living God so long as our accomplishment does not finally put God's will in our possession. The Lord lets us know under what conditions he is prepared to intervene but without our having any guarantee that he will do so, without anything automatic about it, without God being magically tied to it. Now the Holy Spirit who alone gives effect to our life and action is free and sovereign. We are thus completely uncertain as to the possible consequences, and this rules out any calculation or foreknowledge of the future of our acts and our history.

From another angle this acknowledgment of the Holy Spirit forbids any investigation of efficacy as such, as if the Holy Spirit did not exist, as if means alone were enough and we had to find the most efficacious means (which is always possible, since it is true that our means have their own efficacy). The magicians of Pharaoh could do the same miracles as Moses. Yet that which has its own high degree of efficacy should not become legitimate in our eyes for that reason. It is not enough that a means be effective for us to employ it. We must not subordinate the choice of means to intrinsic or specific efficacy.

The effects of the Holy Spirit are of two classes. There are mysterious spiritual effects which we cannot measure and which are found both on earth and in heaven. These are totally his (the birth of faith, the effectiveness of prayer) and will appear visibly only at the end of the age. But this is not the only action of the Holy Spirit. It is an evasion to want to restrict our vision to these effects alone, just as it is a defeat to accept the world's view that we are reduced to this mysterious, hidden, spiritual life. The Holy Spirit also produces effects that are temporal, visible, and concrete. These abound in both the Old Testament and the New. They are effects inscribed on the material world (miracles), on the body, on the moral life (the results of conversion), on psychology, on sociology. These temporal effects are inexplicable apart from the Holy Spirit in spite of man's ever new pretension that he can explain everything on a purely human level (e.g., the history of the church and the origins of Christianity). But here the action and efficacy of the Holy Spirit are integrated into the nexus of the psycho-sociological causes and effects which are their basis, occasion, and expression. As a result the action of the Holy Spirit changes in some sense the course of the world and history without itself alone being history, without making history a mere progression to God or the good, and yet also, reciprocally, without being limited, conditioned, or explained by history. Man is thus summoned to participate in one or other of the actions of the Holy Spirit, in the totality of the work of God. He is summoned to provide the basis for the divine efficacy. In these circumstances, what are the conditions of the efficacy of Christian action? First, it must be an action governed by its objectives, which are themselves subordinate to the end. This seems simple and obvious, but in effect man is much more controlled by his means than his ends. He is much more involved in a causal process. The previous action governs that which follows much more strictly than the project or the ideal. He is conditioned more by the culture to which he is subject from infancy than by the value he seeks to realize. And the more important, demanding, and efficacious means become, the more decisive they are in the choice man makes. He chooses what the means actually allow him to achieve. Now in the perspective of faith it cannot be thus. The objectives to be achieved today are the universal knowledge and enjoyment of the gospel. The end is the coming of the kingdom of God. Everything else must be subordinate, whether at the level of objectives—happiness, science, art, etc.—or at the level of the end—justice, liberty, and peace. The choice of means must be strictly controlled by this perspective. The means must be compatible with the objectives and the end. They must conform and be of the same nature. Hence the gospel cannot be spread by violence or propaganda. If these means are selected, some success may be enjoyed, but it will not be that of the gospel. For the Holy Spirit will give true power and efficacy only to means which are in exact agreement with the actual content of the gospel. There must be intercommunication of means and end if the Holy Spirit is to use our means and invest them with his power. But regard should also be had to the fact that the end is already present in the world, that it is not the result of our activity, that it is here already as a secret force, both evoking and also provoking our means. We have to be obedient to the end, not as a goal to be reached and which we may possess, but also and at the same time as a given fact, something already there, a presence which is active too. Thus hope is an actual reality which makes the ultimate future present and active. Hope actualizes the last days, the *eschaton,* just as faith actualizes the time when Jesus Christ was on the earth as God with us.

Hope is a power which is neither psychological nor of the order of a project. It is not a sentiment that impels us to risk certain things. It gives us no reason to employ such means. It is the presence of the power of the sovereign Christ, of the Christ who is already sovereign and active. This is not of the order of means that are effective. But beyond hope there is also the efficacy, hidden from us, of the kingdom of heaven which is present in the world, mysterious, discernible by none but God. This kingdom of heaven is also at work and its orientation is to the future coming of Christ; it inclines the world to the kingdom of God. And this kingdom of heaven is no longer dependent at all on our means. It *is*. It has its own nature and law, of which the parables in Matthew give us some idea. It is planted by God in the reality of the world. It intervenes by its own decision. Here again we are in the presence of an efficacy which escapes us. In truth it is God who mysteriously and with no visible miracle impels the world towards its fulfilment. Efficacy, then, is as it were the resultant of our means (to which the Holy Spirit gives power), of hope (to which the coming lordship of Jesus Christ gives power), and of the kingdom of heaven hidden in the world. As for us, we can act only at the level of our means. But if our responsibility is total here, this does not have for us the implication either of excessive confidence, of despair, or of the need to choose the most effective means while using others sparingly. If, however, means cannot be invested with power except as they are congruent with the gospel, we are always obliged to raise the question of "why" and "for whom." If, after a searching criticism in this light which screens out anything not pertaining to the "who," our choice of means is determined by its end, it is in the will of God, and one can say, not only that it will bring results, but also that these results were prepared in advance, that God assigned its value in advance, that it enters into the meaning of the ultimate truth of the world, and that it thus shares its efficacy. But in this choice, we must not do what Ahaz did here, i.e., use the means which make possible the attain-

137

ment of an objective quite apart from their effects on the order of truth and love. The implication is that we cannot separate our objectives from the person of Jesus Christ. Peace and justice (and the independence of Israel for Ahaz) have no importance or value in themselves. They are not objectives to be attained in isolation. They have no meaning except as Jesus is the prince of peace, the sun of righteousness, except as Israel is the people of God. Thus any true proclamation of the gospel will entail work for peace, although pacifism both doctrinally and ethically makes no sense and is not intrinsically a serving of Jesus Christ.

This problem of efficacy has, however, another aspect. In Scripture efficacy is always found as a relation. It is the relation of man to God. Man sees that he is relative to God. The relation is that of man as he is first in communion or even union with God. Man's will is in congruity with God's plan. This means that the first step in efficacy is at the level of personal unity. It is when man rediscovers awareness of his authenticity that his action receives an efficacy annexed to it. But on the basis of this personal union all efficacy implies intervention in the historical nexus. There is thus a relation with the state of the world as well. No action can be effective if it is abstracted from the state of the world. This implies a true insertion in history, a continuous and permanent insertion. It seems to me that in this consideration of efficacy the Book of Kings shows us the importance of persistence, of permanence, of renewal, of innovation pursued patiently in the multiplicity of agents and workers. No action is conducted from beginning to end by a single man or means. No one man, not even Elisha, can bear sole responsibility, neither the one who acts nor the one who imparts true efficacy (lest any man should boast, as Paul says). In effect each has to take up his own task and each at his own level has to be responsible for some accomplishment in the conditions already sketched, but the general plan is beyond our vision. As regards effects and results, then, each must rest content with the Lord's promise. Results are promised if we keep to our own level and use the appropriate means. But we cannot ask for more than a promise (such as that made to Elisha and fulfilled after his death). We must not hurry on the fulfilment (Jehu) nor must we appropriate the results, laying hold of them, making them ours, and taking them out of the hand of the Lord (Ahaz). But again, we may say, if all is promise, all is continuity too. Because we cannot ascertain any evident or visible results, we may not stop and rest. If the efficacy of the man of God comes to a halt, all is lost. Jeroboam ruined the kingdom of David. If Apollos had not watered, what Paul had planted would never have grown. Every Christian, then, is strictly accountable, just as there must be continuity in prayer and continuity in effective action. When a Christian quits, he annuls thereby all that preceding Christians have been able to do. Efficacy is written in the history of the church as well as the world. It implies that everyone play his part in the life of the church and be prepared to carry on whether or not there is any tangible proof of results.

If, however, everyone is responsible, we must also realize that it is not for us to organize this continuity nor to institutionalize it. We have to exist *in.* . . . It is this existence which ensures and guarantees both the efficacy and the continuity. We come back to this renouncing or to profiting by the effects or fruits of the actions of the Holy Spirit (the lepers); we can never take possession of them. If Christian action is effective, the effects or fruits are gathered by God and collected by him alone. None of us can boast of them. None can have an individual part. None is the supreme agent of efficacy. Elisha with his word unleashes a Hazael or a Jehu and then withdraws, no longer controlling the situation. But finally we have also to realize that this efficacy will never be evident to the world. The action we attempt will always be regarded by the world as a failure, and the more so the more it is authentically faithful. We cannot be successful or show the church to be effective in the world unless we adopt the world's criterion of efficacy, which means adopting its means as well.

As the world sees it, action which is faithful to God will always fail, just as Jesus Christ necessarily went to the cross. Such action always leads to a dead end. It is always a fiasco from the standpoint of worldly power. But this should not worry us. It does not mean that our action is in truth ineffectual. Efficacy measured in terms of faithfulness cannot be compared at any point with efficacy measured in terms of success.

This is again what the Book of Kings teaches us when it shows us that good and faithful kings were regularly defeated and the glorious monarchs were men like Ahab and Ahaz. These successes, this efficacy as it would be called from man's standpoint, and especially in our own society, will never amount to anything more than the approval given by the world, by society, to certain acts or means. It is the stamp of a group of men, a social body. But if we do not believe that society is good and right, this approval proves nothing except that the action is in conformity with the world. It does not mean at all that the world has changed; quite the contrary. Each time the people of God becomes effective according to the world's criteria, this only implies that society has absorbed our action and is using it to its own ends and for its own profit. This is the way it is between Ahaz and the king of Assyria. The efficacy we think we have is simply a power in the world's service, for the perfecting of its own being, for its better organization. The kingdom of Judah was merely a fulcrum in the general policy of Assyria, a base for the conquest of Egypt. This was what the efficacy of Ahaz finally a-

140

mounted to. In contrast, the efficacy we seek can only be that of a radical alteration of the world and society. It is the efficacy of event as opposed to institution, of tension against the accepted line, of nonconformity. In sum, it is an efficacy which stands opposed to that of the world. Yet it is no less real. It is the efficacy which shatters unanimity, the efficacy of heretics and sectarians. Nor is this negative, for the positive simply cannot exist without it.

Furthermore, in the efficacy which is granted to us by the Holy Spirit there can be no question of securing the approval of the world or its conformity to us. Israel did not have to aim at other nations becoming Israel. Jehu saw this clearly, and so too did David. We have simply to be, and we can only be a question put within the world and to the world, a question invincibly confronting it. This is our efficacy. It is the efficacy of *the* question, a question which society and sociological movements cannot assimilate. Israel and the church have never been efficacious except to the degree that the world has been unable to assimilate them. This is a vocation of the people of God incomparably more authentic than "service" or "works."

It is not at the level of works and their results that this efficacy may be seen; it is at the level of inassimilability. Whenever the church thinks it has succeeded and become great, it is to that degree unfaithful. The adulteration of the church by power, e.g., its social conformity in the Middle Ages, corresponds precisely to the action described here, namely, that of Ahaz. Our only guarantee of efficacy is the achievement of nonconformity. But this is a vocation one cannot take up alone. One can do so only in correlation. One can fulfil this vocation only in relation, as we have tried to show above. In fact it means existing as the incarnate presence of the Wholly Other and at the same time "in-existing" in order that the Wholly Other should not be concealed by our obstinacy, by our worldly efficacy, by our intentions and pretensions. For this in-

141

carnate presence of the Wholly Other at the heart of the world is itself our efficacy. In the last resort this is the only thing that cannot be absorbed, resorbed, and assimilated by the world. No matter how strong our resolve, our means are still the means of the world and they will always participate to some degree in the world. They thus have a hold over us. Society has great power of absorption. Even Solomon could not resist being an oriental monarch when he used the means appropriate thereto. Only the presence of the Wholly Other at the heart of our action cannot be assimilated by sociological forces. It alone is the guarantee of our independence. It evades both society's grip and also our own. The Wholly Other refuses to be used either by the world or by us. In his sovereign freedom, however, he has willingly agreed to go along with us if we will accept his efficacy (which means faithfulness). As we shall soon see, he agrees to go along with Hezekiah. This is our sole efficacy. Since incarnation is at issue, it is the efficacy which leads us, in our relation with the world, to the following challenge: "How can we be the question that God puts to the world?" Elisha was this question unceasingly; Joram, Jehu, and Ahaz were not.

VI

Rabshakeh

2 Kings 18:17-37

17 And the king of Assyria sent (the) Tartan, (the) Rabsaris, and (the) Rabshakeh[1] with a great army from Lachish to King Hezekiah at Jerusalem. And they went up and came to Jerusalem. When they arrived, they came and stood by the conduit of the upper pool, which is on the highway to the Fuller's Field. 18 And when they called for the king, there came out to them Eliakim the son of Hilkiah, who was over the household, and Shebna the secretary, and Joah the son of Asaph, the recorder.

19 And (the) Rabshakeh said to them, "Say to Hezekiah, 'Thus says the great king, the king of Assyria: On what do you rest this confidence of yours? 20 Do you think that mere words are strategy and power for war? On whom do you now rely, that you have rebelled against me? 21 Behold, you are relying now on Egypt, that broken reed of a staff, which will pierce the hand of any man who leans on it. Such is Pharaoh king of Egypt to all who rely on him. 22 But if you say to me, "We rely on the Lord our God," is it not he whose high places and altars Hezekiah has removed, saying to Judah and to Jerusalem, "You shall worship before this altar in Jerusalem"? 23 Come now, make a wager with my master the king of Assyria: I will give you two thousand horses, if you are able on your part to set riders upon them. 24 How then can you repulse a single captain among the least of my master's servants, when you rely on Egypt for chariots and for horsemen? 25 Moreover, is it without the Lord that I have come up against this place to destroy it? The Lord said to me, Go up against this land, and destroy it.' "

---

[1] Modern scholars treat these terms as titles rather than proper names, Tartan as commander-in-chief of the army, Rabsaris as head of the eunuchs, and Rabshakeh as chief cupbearer. This is grammatically possible, but does not make much sense in the context.

26 Then Eliakim the son of Hilkiah, and Shebna, and Joah, said to (the) Rabshakeh, "Pray, speak to your servants in the Aramaic language, for we understand it; do not speak to us in the language of Judah within the hearing of the people who are on the wall." 27 But (the) Rabshakeh said to them, "Has my master sent me to speak these words to your master and to you, and not to the men sitting on the wall, who are doomed with you to eat their own dung and to drink their own urine?"

28 Then (the) Rabshakeh stood and called out in a loud voice in the language of Judah, "Hear the word of the great king, the king of Assyria! 29 Thus says the king: 'Do not let Hezekiah deceive you, for he will not be able to deliver you out of my hand. 30 Do not let Hezekiah make you to rely on the Lord by saying, The Lord will surely deliver us, and this city will not be given into the hand of the king of Assyria.' 31 Do not listen to Hezekiah; for thus says the king of Assyria: 'Make your peace with me and come out to me; then every one of you will eat of his own vine, and every one of his own fig tree, and every one of you will drink the water of his own cistern; 32 until I come and take you away to a land like your own land, a land of grain and wine, a land of bread and vineyards, a land of olive trees and honey, that you may live, and not die. And do not listen to Hezekiah when he misleads you by saying, The Lord will deliver us. 33 Has any of the gods of the nations ever delivered his land out of the hand of the king of Assyria? 34 Where are the gods of Hamath and Arpad? Where are the gods of Sepharvaim, Hena, and Ivvah? Have they delivered Samaria out of my hand? 35 Who among all the gods of the countries have delivered their countries out of my hand, that the Lord should deliver Jerusalem out of my hand?' "

36 But the people were silent and answered him not a word, for the king's command was, "Do not answer him." 37 Then Eliakim the son of Hilkiah, who was over the household, and Shebna the secretary, and Joah the son of Asaph, the recorder, came to Hezekiah with their clothes rent, and told him the words of (the) Rabshakeh.

Ahaz the politician supported the most powerful nation, Assyria, against the weakest nations, Syria and Israel. He helped Assyria to eliminate them. He played his cards as a realistic and effective politician, and won. But he ignored the constant political law that a power which expands rapidly necessarily begins to oppress its allies and becomes

144

increasingly demanding. Ahaz thought he could protect Judah and Jerusalem by his adroit politics. This was true for a time, but in the long run he delivered Jerusalem into the hands of Assyria. This is how it turned out. Assyria no longer had any serious rivals in the area and its ancient ally now became in its eyes a mere servant subject to its orders and without any kind of independence. Any attempt to go its own way was severely punished. About twenty years later Jerusalem itself was besieged under the reign of the son of Ahaz, Hezekiah. During the siege there took place an incident that was commonplace enough in itself. An Assyrian representative, Rabshakeh, came with a deputation to receive the submission of the besieged city. He made two speeches. The first was diplomatic and the second a piece of propaganda. They must have made a great impression, for they have been carefully preserved. They are in fact most remarkable, and in the present series they are an excellent example of the word of the world.[2]

Rabshakeh speaks politically. He says what the political world can and usually will say in confrontation with the church. He is a typical representative of what we are constantly told, and his speeches are of devastating realism. A modern statesman would not need to change a single word. He says precisely what the world says, and this sheds new light on the relation between God and politics.

King Hezekiah sends to meet the Assyrian generals a delegation (even though they had demanded his own presence) consisting of his intendant, secretary, and archivist. The meeting takes place near Jerusalem by the conduit on the road leading to the Fuller's Field. It can be seen from

[2] Perhaps one should not generalize thus and regard Rabshakeh as a representative of the world. The name, which is perhaps a proper name, means literally "chief cupbearer." But I believe it is a richer term than this. According to Davidson the root implies "to become innumerable" and carries with it the sense of power, size, and abundance, an abundance relating to what is both indispensable and ambiguous, i.e., drink, water, or wine.

the walls of Jerusalem. The delegates probably want to negotiate but Rabshakeh asks for unconditional surrender. His speech is theoretically addressed to the delegates alone and is diplomatic in character, but in fact it is spoken in a loud voice in Hebrew, so that the people of Jerusalem on the walls can hear.

I

In fact Rabshakeh has five arguments. He first gives a reminder of what is needed in political action, namely, sagacity and force, calculation and power. The king of Judah has made a bid for independence, but he does not have the material power to resist the king of Assyria, and his political calculations in the search for allies have proved to be wrong. He is a sorry politician; all he has is words. In this context this possibly means that he invokes God or justice or humanity. He perhaps tries to tell the Assyrians what is right and true. But this is all words; in the long run it has no importance. Politics cannot be pursued with mere words. This analysis of the situation in politics is rigorously accurate and we cannot improve on it today. Politics consists of exact calculation and the power to intervene. Rabshakeh is obviously right. Politics cannot rely on values or sentiments. It cannot serve other things. It is measured by the success of what it undertakes. It has its own goal. Those who use it as a means to accomplish something more lofty will either deceive themselves or fail.

Values, sentiments, and opinions are among the given factors which the sagacious calculation of politics will take into account, but there can be no question of achieving justice or truth by politics. These are the illusions of theoreticians, of a king of Judah who trusts in words. In the eyes of the world this kind of thing can be viewed only as words. King Hezekiah is a poor politician. He has miscalculated. He has not been successful in seeking allies to support his revolt against Sennacherib. He is without power. "How then can you repulse a single captain among the least of my master's servants?" The second argument gives greater precision to the thinking of Rabshakeh. It relates to the political mistake of Hezekiah. To try to free himself from the burdensome alliance with Sennacherib, to whom he had to give a large tribute of gold, silver, and slaves, he has turned to the great power in the West, to Egypt, to find the assistance which will counterbalance the power of the East. But Egypt is defeated, and Sennacherib regards the diplomatic maneuvering as open revolt. Hezekiah is thus wrong in thinking that Egypt can give effective help. This is an unpardonable political blunder. Pharaoh is a broken reed which will pierce the hand of any who lean on it. The argument is devastating, for it applies with greater force against Hezekiah than anyone else. In relation to any other king the point of Rabshakeh's speech is limited to what we have said, namely, that there has been here a mistake in military and diplomatic calculation. But in relation to the king of the chosen people. . . .

How many times has God told and retold his people by the prophets that they should not rely on human means. When nourished by manna, they were not to gather and store it as human prudence would dictate. When attacked they were not to trust in arms or numbers. Gideon reduces his army until he has only three hundred men. David rejects the armor, helmet, and sword provided for him by Saul. In famine they were to be ready to lose even what they had in order to receive from God's hand. The widow uses up the last of her flour and oil to feed the prophet; after that they would die. But God's grace is inexhaustible. In spite of all that can be said, in spite of every secular argument to justify money and the state and science and technology, to show that we are right to use these things, it is quite unbiblical to appeal to these agents of political power. To do so is defiance of God *par excellence.* It is to

147

reject God himself. No theological constructions can prevail against the rigor of the choice which God demands and which is not just spiritual and inward. Take no money, nor purse, nor two tunics. . . .

If Hezekiah has been finally defeated, it is because he, the righteous and pious king, the king who is completely faithful, has been unfaithful. And it is again politics which has led him astray from God. Instead of relying on the exclusive power of the Eternal, instead of trusting in the sole Lord and committing himself to his decision, he has organized his little coalition, engaged in his petty diplomacy, and tried to find another ally, the king of Egypt, in addition to God. But this king, as so often, is a broken reed and pierces the hand of the one who relies on this human resource. And Scripture continually shows us that when God's chosen people tries to find other means apart from God to survive, to conquer, to protect itself, then it is attacked and endangered by the very thing in which it trusts. We think of Jonah, or the brazen serpent. Jesus lays down the permanent law in relation to this fact. Where our treasure is, there is our heart also. It is destroyed with the perishable things which the world places at our disposal in order to seduce us and to win our confidence, far away from God and completely outside him. Hezekiah is not just wrong in his political calculations, as politics, too, can show. He has failed to see who his true Lord is. He has relied on human means, valid though these may be, for the problem is not primarily a moral one. This is what Isaiah has told him very forcefully (Isaiah 31:1, 3). The king has already been warned by God.

Hence Rabshakeh puts his finger on the sorest spot without realizing it. He unwittingly pronounces a divine judgment on Hezekiah. It is often thus. In the word it speaks to the church, in its judgments and criticisms, the world often speaks at two levels. In explicit content, and according to its own express intention, what it says is of

148

little worth and simply expresses secular mediocrity. Thus Rabshakeh tells Hezekiah he would have done better to rely on the stronger power of Assyria.

But behind this word, even though the world is unaware of it, there is hidden a profound truth which faith can apprehend because it descries God's intention. Hezekiah knows that he is reproved for having trusted in Egypt, but that he would have been guilty of the same error if he had trusted in Assyria. The reproach of Rabshakeh is true even if wrongly motivated; God's chosen people should not rely on Egypt. Hezekiah, however, sees here more than a lesson in political realism. He grasps the fact that the Lord is his only strength. He also learns the lesson, as we shall see.

It is at this level and within these limits that the church should be infinitely attentive to the criticisms and attacks of unbelievers or enemies. It should not accept their advice or motivation but should look behind this to the judgment which God pronounces on it, and which may be the very opposite of what the world has in view. For the church does not have to follow the logic of the world's political lesson. It must follow God's logic. Thus the obvious conclusion for Rabshakeh is that, since Egypt has proved a false ally, there should be a return to Assyria. But the conclusion for Hezekiah should be that neither Egypt nor Assyria, but God alone, is the one on whom his people must rely. In addition Rabshakeh presents what he regards as the other element in the alternative, and this is his third argument. After the threat he is full of offers and promises. Abandon Egypt and the king of Assyria will shower you with gifts. If Jerusalem surrenders, Rabshakeh in the king's name offers two thousand horses, if, as he ironically adds, there are enough riders to mount them.[3]

The horse was very rare in Israel at this period and the offer to mount a squadron was unexpected. But the im-

[3] The text is uncertain, and there are various translations; we adopt that which seems to make the best sense.

plication is that the king should abase himself before Sennacherib, that he should definitively recognize his suzerainty, and that he should hand over Jerusalem. To the degree that Rabshakeh can see no other possibility, there being only the one choice, his reasoning is cogent and should convince any politician. But to the degree that Hezekiah can hear God's reproach through the lips of the Assyrian, what is offered or proposed is the very thing he cannot accept. He is thrown back irresistibly on God.

Now Rabshakeh obviously does not ignore this possibility. We thus find two other arguments of great importance; they are constantly found in secular discourse. "You may say: It is on Yahweh, our God, that we rely. . . ." A rational politician cannot rely on God; politics is not religion. But Rabshakeh is acquainted with the reforms of Hezekiah.[4] Hezekiah has removed holy things, the Canaanite deities, the brazen serpent which had become an object of worship, the more or less pagan cultic sites. He has re-established the strict cult of Yahweh with only one sanctuary. Now even if the Assyrian knows of the reforms he is fundamentally unable to understand them. How can you trust in the true God when you have just done things displeasing to all gods? You have broken down altars, destroyed statues, and suppressed holy things. God has to be jealous for holy things. The Assyrian evidently thinks in terms of a divine solidarity familiar to the people of his age. In his view, since these altars and statues were in the territory of Judah, the local god was bound to be interested and involved at this point. This was an attack on him. What he cannot understand is that Yahweh is not a God like all the rest, that he is in fact a Wholly Other, that he is not subject to the common measure, and that when he confronts what men call god the only possible issue is

[4] Some historians think that only Josiah carried through these reforms a century later. But even if we have here a later addition, which is by no means obvious, what counts is the significance of Rabshakeh's speech.

the annihilation of the gods. We have here a constant misconception on the part of the world. The natural man has to live. He cannot see the importance of truth. He can only scoff at theological debates, at the Byzantines. He cannot attach any importance to the inner life of the church. He reproaches the church for concerning itself with theology when there are so many good works to do. The world makes the same realistic speech as Rabshakeh: "Do not cast your gaze on God; look at the reality of the world. In any case, you have displeased this God. He is against you. He will not come to your aid." Here again we have a speech compounded of truth and illusion. The reason Rabshakeh advances is ridiculous and shows in effect that the natural man has no understanding, like twentieth-century man, who finds some Protestants more acceptable because they at least do not believe in stupid miracles, in the nativity and the resurrection!

But Hezekiah himself has to see a truth here. Yahweh is even more demanding. What has been done is not yet enough to show how different he is. If the reform had been more radical, perhaps the pagan would have begun to see that God is indeed wholly other. When criticized by the world, the church does not have to agree that the world is right and that it must take part in social and political action as the world advises. What it must see is that it has not been able to show with sufficient intransigence, rigor, absoluteness, holiness, and separateness, how different God is. If Rabshakeh can confuse God and the gods at this point, it is because Hezekiah has not gone far enough in his break with the world. This is what the church should tell itself as it listens to the criticisms of the world, which wants it to serve a kindly God who is practical, utilitarian, and progressive.

Poor Rabshakeh, how mistaken he is, and especially when he thinks the Lord will assuredly not come to the aid of a people that has displeased him! He measures God by the standard of his own false gods and personal ideas. It is true that everything in this world avenges itself, that every offense has to be paid for, that every insult to the gods leads to death, especially if this god is the king. But Rabshakeh does not know the Lord. The Lord is not like others. He is rich in goodness, full of compassion and mercy. He does not will that the sinner should perish. How could the Assyrian know that even if God has been offended, nevertheless he will not abandon his people? He will defend it just the same. He will save it and heal it. Rabshakeh's theological reasoning is of no value. The church has nothing to learn from the world regarding the God who is the true God. The world can speak only about its experience and wisdom and limits and interpretation of the divine. This is not to be despised, but it has nothing to do with God. The only thing is that the wise or solemn declarations of the world about God can disturb Israel, the church, and the Christian. They can lead them astray. They can cause them to confuse the God of Abraham, Isaac, and Jacob, who was in Jesus Christ, with all that the world is talking about. This, as we have seen, was the confusion of which Jeroboam was guilty. And this ambiguity leads to the final argument of Rabshakeh, the irresistible argument: "Is it without the Lord that I have come up against this place to destroy it? The Lord said to me, Go up against this land, and destroy it." This is a logical continuation of the previous point. You have displeased your God, and your God has thus sent me to destroy you.

Rabshakeh admits the existence of this God. His pantheon is not exclusive. He refers to this God. He even allows that Yahweh is the God of the land or territory. It is with his permission and at his command that things have reached this pass. From the Assyrian's standpoint there is nothing derisive or hypocritical about this saying. But the question he puts is the most terrible one a non-Christian can put to a Christian. Is it God's will that wars should come, that Hitler should rise to power, that communism should obliterate Christianity in China? The argument is the classical one. Either God is omnipotent and creates evil, or he is not omnipotent. . . .

In any case, this argument is designed to shatter completely the confidence of Israel. For it is true that God has commanded Assyria to invade Judah. The scourge of God who mocks God's will is still speaking the truth when he claims to be the scourge of God. The error here is that of using God in the speech, of making him a tool of propaganda, of trying to exploit him. Here again what the world says about God is radically mistaken even though it expresses something which Israel must see to be true and contains a very profound truth which Rabshakeh himself does not believe. But when this profound truth, which is confirmed by the prophet Isaiah, is received and heard, should it lead to psychological collapse, to surrender and passivity? In other words, even if the Assyrian is in effect the scourge of God, does this mean that to fight against him is to fight against God? The argument is often heard that misery is a test imposed by God and so the wretches who suffer it must not revolt. Hitler is God's scourge and so he must not be resisted. We hear the same today regarding communism. What we forget is that in such matters God's aim is not a political one. The point is not at all that Assyria or Germany should become a great nation, nor that the economic system should be socialist. God uses the Assyrian in order that his people should really become his people again in truth, in humility, in sanctity, in authenticity. What happens has to do with Israel or the church, and not the state or capitalism or socialism. To repent and to accept the punishment does not at all imply passivity. Once God's intention is perceived and accepted, then in faith, and in virtue of faith, there is need, politically, to act against the one who shows himself to be God's enemy.

Poor Rabshakeh, at this point too he fails to see that

this God is not like his own gods, that the Lord does not punish forever, that he not only unleashes the scourge but also holds it back, that he finds no satisfaction in the Assyrian terror and the church's misery, that he does not will the death of the sinner and hence does not will the final victory of Assyria. It is true that the conqueror has come thus far by God's will, and that he can proclaim this. But what he does not know is that he can go no further, that his limit has already been reached. For what he fails to see is that he himself is only an instrument in God's hands in his relation to Israel, the church. In other spheres he may have a great measure of autonomy or independence. But here he is only a chopper, and can the chopper vaunt itself when in the hands of the woodcutter? It is one thing when the state is in its own domain and quite another when it is in positive or negative confrontation with the church. Here the autonomy of power is strictly controlled by the intention of God for his people. But to know this and to believe it there is need of total commitment to God, of repentance, of acceptance of God's will, of readiness to see it through to the end. "If it be possible, let this cup pass from me; nevertheless, not as I will, but as thou wilt" (Matthew 26:39). This is where the concrete question is bound to arise, and how often do we hear it in the Psalms and Revelation: "O Sovereign Lord . . . how long . . . ?" (Revelation 6:10). For we do not know in advance where God has set the limit. We do not know where the scourge will halt. Only faith and repentance can give at one and the same time both the patience to endure and also the courage to fight the invader. But for others the argument is terribly convincing and even decisive. For Israel it is a reason for yielding, for surrender. This is why, when Israel's envoys hear this terrible argument, they ask Rabshakeh to speak in Aramaic (the common language of the Middle East, but a language which at this period was not yet generally understood in Israel). They, the responsible ones, can listen to this argument and not be shaken by it. But they are afraid of its psychological impact on the crowd which is massed on the walls and which can also hear it. They have little confidence in the faith and solidity of the masses. They think the arguments of Rabshakeh are strong enough to sway them.

II

But when Rabshakeh sees their fears he redoubles his efforts and makes another speech which is much cruder but which is a good specimen of propaganda. He now addresses the crowd directly with a view to bringing about the movement that will lead to surrender. He begins by reminding the people of their miserable condition, of the famine, and he insists that they are in desperate straits. Then come three modes of psychological action which remind us of modern propaganda. His first aim is to separate the crowd from the leaders. "Hezekiah is deceiving you. Do not listen to Hezekiah." This is a classical device, to shake the confidence of the masses in their political rulers, to accuse the head of state, to make oneself out to be a liberator. "Hezekiah is deceiving you but we are men of good faith. Hezekiah is using the devices of propaganda to lead you astray (v. 32) but I who now speak to you am absolutely honest. Again, we are not fighting against the people of Israel but only against the clique of king, heads, and rulers. Once you get rid of these (and you should do this yourselves), then peace will reign."

This is familiar political propaganda, but we should remember that it is also the traditional position of the world in relation to the church. "Poor people, exploited by horrible priests and monks. Look at the wealth of bishops and the corpulence of canons while you faint with hunger. You are led astray by stories and fables. You are

155

indoctrinated by theology, the catechism, and faith in general. We have now come to set you free." (It should not be forgotten that in modern times Napoleon and Hitler are among those who have taken to themselves the title of liberator.) "We are honest. We have no self-interest in telling you this. But those who keep you in the servitude of faith really do so for sordid selfish reasons." And when the world begins a religious persecution, whether it be the Convention, Napoleon, Hitler, Stalin, Rajk, or Castro, it is never aimed against poor believers, whose good they are really seeking, but always against a clique of exploiters of Christianity. Nor is the reason for it found in hostility to the faith but rather in the fact that this clique is against the regime, is engaged in a plot, is supporting international Jewry, or is fighting for the great capitalists.

Rabshakeh's speech is frighteningly modern. This ought to be a reminder that it discloses what will always be the world's attitude to the church and what arguments will be used to the end of history in the world's case against it. The charge which tries to divide the confessors of the faith or guides of the flock from the general assembly of God's people, so that the latter become as sheep without a shepherd and as men carried about with every wind of doctrine, is remarkably successful even to our own day.

The denunciation of bad rulers is then followed by the promise: "If you throw off the king (priests, the church, etc.), if you make peace with me, Rabshakeh, the world, then you will be happy. Every one of you will eat of his own vine . . . and I will take you away to a rich and plentiful land where you will live a good life. In fact, if you are hungry and miserable, if you cannot eat of the fruit of your vine, it is the fault of the exploiters and of the church which is on the side of the exploiters. But if you leave the faith, if you stop putting your hope in a future which is promised by God but which is a mere illusion, if you will make a pact with me and work for

156

me—the prince of the world—then you will find happiness. I will lead you into a land of affluence. You will live and not die. . . ." We recognize again the argument of anti-Christian propaganda. There is nothing new here. "All these I will give you, if you will fall down and worship me" (Matthew 4:9). From Eden on we know how much this promise is worth, and yet it always succeeds. Whether for power or for happiness man is always ready to leave his Lord. The argument is particularly devastating today, for it is addressed precisely to the deprived, to workers, to those who live in underdeveloped countries (who are in even worse case than the besieged in Jerusalem), and it is true enough on its negative side. There really are exploiters. There is an oppressive elite. This was true in Israel in the days of Rabshakeh. At this very time Micah was vigorously denouncing injustice, hoarding, and the exploitation of the poor. Women were being driven out of their homes, the poor were being stripped of their very skin, and the princes of the house of Israel were perverting the law. They were building Jerusalem with wrong, while the prophets were prophesying for money (Micah 3-4). Thus moral collapse and social injustice characterized Jerusalem and the chosen people. Rabshakeh's speech rests on accurate data. His propaganda is aimed at a people which has experienced all this. This is why his argument is so strong. This is also why what I have written above does not mean that the church is right and good and that the world is attacking it unjustly. The world's propaganda against Christians and the church states things which are incontestably true. Like all good propaganda, the attack on the church is well supported. But like all propaganda it is radically false. It is untrue on two counts: first as regards the promises of Rabshakeh, and then as regards his honesty. For, although he claims that the church lies and he does not, Rabshakeh also lies, for his promises are false and are merely a trap.

When he says the church is on the side of the oppressors

and he comes to bring happiness he is lying, for he is a worse oppressor than any before him. While it is true that the poor in Israel are being exploited by the rich, it is also true that when they have been conquered and deported they will be exploited far worse. If they have been enslaved by the great, when they are in the hands of strangers they will be enslaved far worse. "I will take you to an affluent land. . . ." But we know how the kings of Assyria treated conquered peoples. The skins of carved up people covered the walls of the palaces. This is the promised happiness. Here is the lie in the propaganda which the world uses to try to detach men from the church.

A second lie relates to the injustices in Israel on the basis of which Rabshakeh seeks to induce the people to renounce its God. This is once again the traditional line. "Christians are unworthy. It is easy to prove this. The church is not the kingdom of God. God does not exist. Do not let yourselves be deluded into living by faith. God will not save. God will not console. God will not revive. Those who make these fair promises are merely speaking empty words. It is in their own interests and for their own advantage that they speak about God (and in fact God can be a good propaganda point, and Hezekiah was the first to be threatened, and he would not listen to Sennacherib but insisted that Jerusalem should hold out to the last). The aim is to keep you in bondage and exploitation (we note in passing that this is the serpent's charge against God himself). Stop looking forward to a future fashioned by God. Make your own future, or rather, trust Sennacherib to make it for you. Stop looking to heaven for deliverance and the establishment of justice. It is within your reach. Simply surrender and bow before the might of the world. Stop believing in this useless God and make reasonable decisions which can be calculated on the human level." This is how Rabshakeh continues in forceful and realistic terms.

And now comes the usual conclusion which is designed to bring the besieged to their knees. God does not will to deliver you. It is not now because of the wickedness of the great that Israel or Christians should turn from God. The world progresses by attacking God himself. And the Assyrian argument is just the same as that used today. This God of whom you speak is just like the gods of all the nations. What have these gods been able to do against the conqueror? Has any of them saved his land from the hands of the king of Assyria? Where are the gods of Hamath and Arpad, of Sepharvaim, Hena, and Ivvah? They have been swept away along with those who believed in them. Yahweh is no greater than any of these. Why should he be able to save Jerusalem? How often have we heard this? The gods of the Polynesians or Bantus could not protect these peoples. These gods were man's creation, the product of his culture. They perished when men ceased to believe in them. Hence things happened quite apart from them. The same applies to Jesus Christ. In dechristianized nations things go just as well and even, strictly speaking, better. What actually remains, the only enduring reality, is the greatness of man, who creates gods and destroys them. Has anything been done with God's help as great as the miracles performed by man with science once he has divested himself of God? The story of man is strewn with the corpses of his gods just as the victorious march of Sennacherib was littered with shattered idols. It is now the turn of Jesus Christ. Know your age. Your age is that of the glory of Sennacherib, the glory of man. One can relate the two exactly, for the most modern statement is just the same as that of the victorious Assyrian: "It is by the force of my hand that I have acted. It is by my own wisdom. For I am intelligent. I have pushed back the frontiers of the world. Like a hero, I have overthrown all that was seated on a throne. I have gathered all the earth" (Isaiah 10:12-14). Were these words really written in the seventh century B.C.? Do they not sum up the whole thinking of modern man? And when Rabshakeh shows the besieged the futility of their faith and the uselessness of their prayers, we have precisely the same situation as that which obtains today when the church is besieged by the world. Rabshakeh bases his case on facts: the brilliant victories and Assyrian might. The world bases its case on facts: the miracles of science and progress. The aim is the same, namely, that Jerusalem should accept these reasonable and obvious arguments, that Christians should follow in the train of the world. There is no alternative. Politics has led us to generalize the problem, for it is in reality general, but politics is the point where opposition crystallizes, and all the powers allied against the Lord meet at this point.

III

Confronted by this propaganda address, the people is silent. We are not told that it remains untouched or unmoved, or that it is not tempted to go along with Rabshakeh. It undoubtedly is. This is inevitable. But it has received orders from the king to say nothing, to give no answer, whether in the form of polemic or in that of dialogue. This again is full of good sense. It is full of good sense, this act of a defeated and hungry people which still has confidence in its king and obeys his orders. It would be well for the broken church with which we are familiar today, for the people of God, if it could still trust in its leaders and accept their advice and respect them. When the world attacks the church in this way, when the state launches its offensive, silence alone is legitimate. Within the church today there is too much preoccupation with "not making proselytes" or "not engaging in apologetics," as though we were still in the age of a socially triumphant church using propaganda against poor and defenseless innocents. This view of the situation is outdated. In fact the church is now the prey of propaganda. It is assaulted by political propaganda. But in this new situation polemics and apologetics are no longer legitimate. In face of the propaganda with which the world attacks the church, the church can only keep silence, for no true witness to God is now possible. No reply can be given to Rabshakeh. Whatever one might say would have no meaning for him. Propaganda interdicts all witness to the Lord. The use of propaganda is contrary to the declaration of the gospel. Counter-propaganda cannot be used against the man who himself uses propaganda. The only way the church can take is that of silence. Silence and not dialogue! I have often said that the Christian's vocation in the world, and especially in politics, is that of dialogue, not merely the dialogue of Christian and unbeliever, which is banal, but the dialogue of enemies and of those who do not understand one another, in which the Christian can play the role of bridge or interpreter, helping them to understand one another. But this dialogue cannot be initiated no matter how or at what cost.

With a glorious and powerful figure who seeks to detach us from our God, to ensure the triumph of the world, to use propaganda to revive the temptation with which Jesus was tempted, to bring the church under submission to money or the state, there is no dialogue, for dialogue is not a value of its own and is not the supreme expression of the Christian life. The only option in such a case is silence, and, as we shall soon see, repentance and prayer. No, dialogue is not to be undertaken no matter when or with whom. Rabshakeh is barred from dialogue with the people of God. There is a time for speech and a time for silence, says Ecclesiastes (3:7). We shall often have occasion to meditate on this.

VII

Hezekiah

2 Kings 19

1　When King Hezekiah heard it, he rent his clothes, and covered himself with sackcloth, and went into the house of the Lord. 2　And he sent Eliakim, who was over the household, and Shebna the secretary, and the senior priests, covered with sackcloth, to the prophet Isaiah the son of Amoz. 3　They said to him, "Thus says Hezekiah, This day is a day of distress, of rebuke, and of disgrace; children have come to the birth, and there is no strength to bring them forth. 4　It may be that the Lord your God heard all the words of (the) Rabshakeh, whom his master the king of Assyria has sent to mock the living God, and will rebuke the words which the Lord your God has heard; therefore lift up your prayer for the remnant that is left." 5　When the servants of King Hezekiah came to Isaiah, 6　Isaiah said to them, "Say to your master, 'Thus says the Lord: Do not be afraid because of the words that you have heard, with which the servants of the king of Assyria have reviled me. 7　Behold, I will put a spirit in him, so that he shall hear a rumor and return to his own land; and I will cause him to fall by the sword in his own land.' "

8　(The) Rabshakeh returned, and found the king of Assyria fighting against Libnah; for he heard that the king had left Lachish. 9　And when the king heard concerning Tirhakah king of Ethiopia, "Behold, he has set out to fight against you," he sent messengers again to Hezekiah, saying, 10　"Thus shall you speak to Hezekiah king of Judah: 'Do not let your God on whom you rely deceive you by promising that Jerusalem will not be given into the hand of the king of Assyria. 11　Behold, you have heard what the kings of Assyria have done to all lands, destroying them utterly. And shall you be delivered? 12　Have the gods of the nations delivered them, the nations which my fathers destroyed, Gozan, Haran, Rezeph, and the people of Eden who were in Tel-assar? 13 Where is the king of Hamath, the king of Arpad, the king of the city of Sepharvaim, the king of Hena, or the king of Ivvah?'"

14 Hezekiah received the letter from the hand of the messengers, and read it; and Hezekiah went up to the house of the Lord, and spread it before the Lord. 15 And Hezekiah prayed before the Lord, and said: "O Lord, the God of Israel, who art enthroned above the cherubim, thou art the God, thou alone, of all the kingdoms of the earth; thou hast made heaven and earth. 16 Incline thy ear, O Lord, and hear; open thy eyes, O Lord, and see; and hear the words of Sennacherib, which he has sent to mock the living God. 17 Of a truth, O Lord, the kings of Assyria have laid waste the nations and their lands, 18 and have cast their gods into the fire; for they were no gods, but the work of men's hands, wood and stone; therefore they were destroyed. 19 So now, O Lord our God, save us, I beseech thee, from his hand, that all the kingdoms of the earth may know that thou, O Lord, art God alone."

20 Then Isaiah the son of Amoz sent to Hezekiah, saying, "Thus says the Lord, the God of Israel: Your prayer to me about Sennacherib king of Assyria I have heard. 21 This is the word that the Lord has spoken concerning him:

"She despises you, she scorns you—
    the virgin daughter of Zion;
she wags her head behind you—
    the daughter of Jerusalem.
22 "Whom have you mocked and reviled?
    Against whom have you raised your voice
and haughtily lifted your eyes?
    Against the Holy One of Israel!
23 By your messengers you have mocked the Lord,
    and you have said, 'With my many chariots
I have gone up the heights of the mountains,
    to the far recesses of Lebanon;
I felled its tallest cedars,
    its choicest cypresses;
I entered its farthest retreat,
    its densest forest.
24 I dug wells
    and drank foreign waters,
and I dried up with the sole of my foot
    all the streams of Egypt.'
25 "Have you not heard
    that I determined it long ago?

I planned from days of old
  what now I bring to pass,
that you should turn fortified cities into heaps of ruins,
26 while their inhabitants, shorn of strength,
    are dismayed and confounded,
  and have become like plants of the field,
    and like tender grass,
  like grass on the housetops;
    blighted before it is grown?
27 "But I know your sitting down
    and your going out and coming in,
    and your raging against me.
28 Because you have raged against me
    and your arrogance has come into my ears,
  I will put my hook in your nose
    and my bit in your mouth,
  And I will turn you back on the way by which you came.

29 "And this shall be the sign for you: this year you shall eat what grows of itself, and in the second year what springs of the same; then in the third year sow, and reap, and plant vineyards, and eat their fruit. 30 And the surviving remnant of the house of Judah shall again take root downward, and bear fruit upward; 31 for out of Jerusalem shall go forth a remnant, and out of Mount Zion a band of survivors. The zeal of the Lord will do this.

32 "Therefore thus says the Lord concerning the king of Assyria, He shall not come into this city or shoot an arrow there, or come before it with a shield or cast up a siege mound against it. 33 By the way that he came, by the same he shall return, and he shall not come into this city, says the Lord. 34 For I will defend this city to save it, for my own sake and for the sake of my servant David."

35 And that night the angel of the Lord went forth, and slew a hundred and eighty-five thousand in the camp of the Assyrians; and when men arose early in the morning, behold, these were all dead bodies. 36 Then Sennacherib king of Assyria departed, and went home, and dwelt at Nineveh. 37 And as he was worshiping in the house of Nisroch his god, Adram-melech and Sharezer, his sons, slew him with the sword, and escaped into the land of Ararat. And Esarhaddon his son reigned in his stead.

This chapter opens with a pitiable scene. In face of the besieging Assyrian army and the extraordinary speech of Rabshakeh, the king cuts a sorry figure. He tears his clothes, a classical sign of despair. We have seen that Joram did the same in similar circumstances in Samaria. And yet, instead of making a fine rejoinder, or addressing a fiery appeal to his people, or making haste to strengthen the weak points in the defenses, or considering the possibilities of getting fresh supplies, or making a supreme military effort, or perhaps engaging in the most skillful possible negotiations, Hezekiah takes refuge in the temple and sends messengers to Isaiah. In other words, he does the very opposite of what a Jehu or an Ahaz would have done. From a realistic standpoint, we cannot fail to find this attitude very weak, cowardly, and irresponsible. For the task of a king is surely to defend his people and to use material means to do so. We seem to have here the typical retreat of the Christian from reality. It is the attitude which is so often attacked. The Christian is a coward who when confronted by difficulties takes refuge in the bosom of his God, in false hopes and an illusory protection. This is what Marxists regard as ideological opium and psychologists as infantile regression and sociologists as artificial cultural reassurance. But in face of these human judgments Scripture speaks differently, and perhaps it would be as well to listen to it.

I

Joram rent his garments and gave way to despair in face of the moral horror of the fact which was revealed to him and his powerlessness to make any reply. But Hezekiah performs the same act for different reasons. It is not because the siege is hard, for the situation is no worse today than yesterday. It is not because the situation is hopeless nor because he fears the effects of the propaganda. The people stands firm and obeys him; the propaganda has failed. When then? His only reason is that the king of Assyria has mocked the living God. This is the essential point. Hezekiah tears his clothes in anger and indignation and in despair that the Lord can be thus insulted by men. It is a day of anguish because man is making a direct assault on God. It is a day when babies are ready to be born and there is no strength to deliver them, for the living God, who gives force and life, has been insulted. After this, there is in fact nothing more to be done. For, political though the problem may be, it is no longer a political affair. It has a dimension which is more than political. And the king, the political head, can do no more. He may fight or negotiate, but this is no longer the problem. God has been called an idol. It has been said that he is not above the gods of other nations. It has been dubbed an illusion to believe that God is a God who saves rather than destroys. At issue now is God's honor. This is the true problem. Hezekiah now shows himself to be an exemplary king because he is one of those very rare rulers who knows the limits of politics. Man can do many things, but there is a limit. And when this limit, which is God's honor, is reached by man, there is a twofold temptation, either on the one side to pass the limit, to take up God's cause, to try to avenge God's honor oneself, to use political means in the service of the living God in order to do this, or on the other side to remain within the limit but to continue political action as though it did not exist, in other words, to separate the two kingdoms, to argue that while God's honor is there at the limit of politics, and I can do nothing about it, nevertheless in my own sphere I can still act like a shrewd and effective man, pursuing politics to save what can be saved by human means. Now the correctness of Hezekiah's attitude is that he understands that when God's honor is in any way involved in the attack of the world it is not for man to make it his own cause. But he also perceives that at this point one cannot separate the two kingdoms. In other words, there is a "suspension of the political." We have already had occasion to note a "suspension of the ethical." We now see another aspect of the same problem. Transgression of the limit, direct provocation of God, brings about the annulment of all possible politics, positive or negative. It robs political action of all meaning. To take up a position in the sphere of human action is futile, for in the strict sense this no longer has significance or content. It might be good for us to consider this phenomenon, for possibly we are in precisely a period like this today. At this point the totality of action, including political action, can consist only in going into the house of the Lord and turning to the prophet. The king can no longer be king in these conditions. He puts everything in a prophet's hands. He does precisely what Joram and Ahaz refused to do, and we have seen the result of this refusal.

From this moment on the story develops in two stages. The king has laid hold of the prophet, and the latter replies with a prophetic word of comfort. God has noted the outrage. He will make the king of Assyria withdraw. This takes place. Sennacherib receives news of a military threat in the south. He has to take swift action against the king of Ethiopia, to defeat him, and then to return to Jerusalem. And Sennacherib restates his will, and repeats his affirmation and insult. He writes to the king of Judah: "Do not imagine that because I have partly raised the siege you have carried the day. I will come back and this will be the end." Nor does he content himself with this threat. One aspect of the letter is very remarkable, for it centers on the problem of God's action: "Do not think that God will deliver you." He repeats the arguments of Rabshakeh: All the nations have been conquered in spite of their gods. Possibly Sennacherib had heard that the people of Jerusalem saw a divine miracle in Tirhakah's attack, or that it was following the common idea of the age, namely, that all events are due to divine intervention, this included. Why, then, should it not be from Yahweh? Either way, Sennacherib wants to dispel the illusion. He reaffirms his view that human might is superior to God. When Hezekiah receives the letter, he thus perceives that the Assyrian refuses to see God's hand in this event. He perceives that the man who will not see in this a sign, and who says so expressly, is a man whose eyes are closed.

This man will not accept that the event is from God. God is not to be mixed up in politics. Isaiah has announced the sign, and it has come to pass, but the one most closely involved will not regard it as such. It has not led him to repent of his insult to God. On the contrary, he renews the insult. Hence Hezekiah can do nothing but turn directly to God. It is not enough even to act through the prophet as an intermediary. Hezekiah goes up to the temple, the letter of the king of Assyria in his hand, and presents the matter to God. The important thing at this point is that he does not ask for victory. He does not pray that the king of Assyria be destroyed. His prayer is in reality a confession of faith: "Thou art the God, thou alone, of all the kingdoms of the earth." This is the positive thing he opposes to the attitude of the Assyrian king. He does not compare his own fidelity to the latter's illusion. He simply affirms his faith in the sole Lord. At this moment the difference is established even though he is at no pains to establish it himself.

Before God he opposes his faith to the derision with which God is attacked. There is no debate. No rational proof is advanced. He does not try to demonstrate in any way the distinction between God and idols. And if we recall that the speech of Rabshakeh is typical of all the addresses in which the men of our own day attack God, it is important to realize that we cannot reply by any philosophy, or experience, or science. The only answer of Hezekiah is a prayer which contains a confession of faith. Hezekiah notes that what the Assyrian says is true. He has indeed defeated all the nations and destroyed their gods. Similarly, the speeches of modern man express a reality. God is dead, Christianity is checked, Christendom is in a state of dissolution, religion is linked to a certain stage in the evolution of the human spirit. There is a measure of truth in all this. And in face of it, we can only affirm with Hezekiah that "these were no gods" and that no god is like unto Thee. Whatever men may say bears no reference to the God and Father of Jesus Christ. I cannot prove this, but I know it in the same way as I know that I myself am alive. And finally, if Hezekiah prays that Israel may be delivered, it is not in order to gain the victory, or to enjoy political success, or to take vengeance on the Assyrian, but "that all the kingdoms of the earth may know that thou, O Lord, art God alone." The glory of God is the only answer to the insult paid to God's honor. The political act which is from God alone must show in an incontestable way to what degree God is the Lord, and the limited faith of Jerusalem and the church can only be the occasion by which the sovereignty of God over all nations is recognized. This is how God's universality can be proclaimed, and not just proclaimed but demonstrated, for God alone can demonstrate his universality. It is not to be seen in the expansion of the church, or in the diaspora, or in the triumph of Christian civilization, or in the impressing of our forces into God's service. Nevertheless, the problem is a political one. It is no mere matter of friendly rhetoric or academic dialogue or an inner spiritual adventure. Everything is political here, the siege, the famine, the war, the carving up of the vanquished, the balance of power between Egypt and Assyria.

Everything is political, but the genius and truth of Hezekiah is to have seen behind the political problem the real question: "Who is the Lord?" To be sure, the question seems to us to be very banal. Every Christian will say easily and smoothly and almost out of habit: "The Lord Jesus

Christ." But what is needed to make this correct answer a true one is the political dimension. To say that God is the Lord when Sennacherib is about to enslave you and put out your eyes is to say something of real significance. Similarly today, we have to ask whether technics, happiness, the state, money, or communism (our modern Sennacheribs) must be called the Lord or (there can be no question of an "and") whether Jesus Christ is Lord. "No one can serve two masters" (Matthew 6:24). If we constantly try to work out optimistic syntheses and happy reconciliations it is because we have not yet seen that we are besieged no less severely than Hezekiah was by our comforts and our economic systems and our political convictions. It is because we have not yet seen that every party and every nation will try to do to the church as Sennacherib did to Israel, namely, to shut it up like a bird in a cage. But at the same time we receive from these powers the same reassurances as Rabshakeh gave to Hezekiah. The only problem, however, is this: "Who is the Lord of the nations?" Now at this level it is impossible to give a political answer to the question. From the very outset a political answer is futile, inconsistent, and inadequate. For we are confronted here by two absolute claims of which the political claim is one. When politics makes an absolute claim, the reply cannot be made on the political plane. So long as the political debate is within the relative sphere, the Christian can play a part with his own proper methods and forces and his own responsibility, as we have seen already. But when one of the powers claims to be God, to embrace the totality of human life, to give total meaning to action, history and life, no relation is possible, not even that of conflict, for here one absolute claim can be met only by another absolute claim. In the presence of one who claims to be God, victory can go only to another who claims to be God. Communism alone can defeat National Socialism or *vice versa,* and that by the use of the same means. If in these circumstances the Christian intervenes in the political debate, his only option is to launch a crusade in the name of Christ the King, a Christ who has become an absolute political power in the hands of men.

The Christian must not enter into this debate, for in face of the absolute claim of politics the only answer is the absolute manifestation of God. This must come, but God acts only when believers act, and the act of believers at this point is the refusal to act to which we have just referred. At this point political action consists in withdrawing into the house of the Lord and crying to him. At this point serious presence in the world can only take the form of reaffirmation of the truth of God, of faith in the Lord of the nations and the Father of Jesus Christ. If we are not mistaken, this is the most difficult course.

It is difficult because this attitude seems to be one of passivity when action appears to be most necessary; in a war or a revolution it is much more difficult to pray than to fire guns. It is difficult because it will arouse universal hostility at such a time; everyone is espousing absolute options and there is general condemnation of the man who withdraws into the house of the Lord. He is cowardly, weak, fearful, and useless. It is hard to accept judgments of this kind. There is also an element of danger, for the one who adopts this attitude seems to be the enemy of every warring power, will not be protected by any group or human force, and will be executed no matter who wins. We should also bear in mind that this attitude is justifiable only when politics presses its claim to the limit. Yet this situation is much more common today than we often think. We have only to remember how similar Rabshakeh's speech is to the innumerable speeches we are constantly hearing.

II

Next, God acts, and we have here a remarkable sequence. First he gives a warning, then he pronounces a judgment which is formulated by his prophet, and finally there comes the miraculous and shattering execution.

We have already mentioned the warning. The king of Ethiopia advances against Assyria. God provokes a political move and the king of Assyria is forced to meet the threat. He should have seen that this was not just the result of chance or of simple political calculation. He should have seen that he was biting off more than he could chew. But he did not see this. We need not pursue this further.

In face of the clear prayer of Hezekiah, God sends an answer through his prophet. His judgment is pronounced. It should be noted that although this is a sure and certain judgment on the Assyrian, it is revealed to God's people, to Israel. Today when everyone seems to be talking about the high value and positive significance of the world, it is perhaps out of place to recall that there is a judgment on the power of the world and of man. Today when everyone seems to be talking about the uselessness and negative stance of the church, it is perhaps out of place to recall that revelation is given to the church alone, and that this revelation includes the judgment on the world, on Babylon and its science and its grandeur. Our text is imperative. In the revelation of this judgment which is given to Israel the dimension is not just that of hope and consolation. God simply says to Hezekiah: "Your prayer . . . I have heard." He does not begin by telling him that things will work out, that he will be the victor, that he will be delivered. He does this the first time, in the warning, at the level of simple political events. At this first stage God says in effect: "Do not be afraid because of the words that you have heard . . . he shall return to his own land." He comforts Hezekiah and tells him the siege will be raised. But now things have gone much further. The problem is no longer the siege of Jerusalem and the sorry plight of God's people. At issue now is the pride of man, his claim to be God, his exaltation. In the prophecy, even though it is revealed to

172

the people of Israel and pronounced within the walls of Jerusalem, the "thou" which God utters is addressed to the Assyrian. God speaks to this Assyrian even though he does so among his own people. The "thou" which is uttered, and which was never perhaps addressed directly to Sennacherib by a human voice, is said in eternity, and it is of little significance whether a messenger comes to address it to the one accused. God's sovereignty is expressed in this act too, namely, in the fact that the accused is condemned without any chance to defend himself. But he has been warned. This Assyrian has engaged in a vast enterprise. "With my many chariots I have gone up the heights of the mountains." He has vanquished nature, brought creation under subjection, imposed his dominion on forests, mountains, and rivers. He can check rivers in their flow and annihilate forests. He has only to pass over a place, to set the sole of his foot there, and the world belongs to him and is transformed. It is worth noting that in verses 23-24 the reference is not to wars and massacres but to man's domination of nature, which was certainly a result of the Assyrian's military success but which was also a greater sign of supremacy. Man, of course, is like one of the natural objects in the hands of man: "Their inhabitants, shorn of strength, are dismayed and confounded, and have become like plants of the field, and like tender grass, like grass on the housetops. . . ." What is forgotten is that when the power of man is unleashed it is never in the hands of all men ("man" here means some men rather than all men, and this is even more flagrantly so today). It is in the hands of a small number of men for whom other men are objects to be treated as the means of power, as natural factors. Now this greatness and power, as we are clearly shown, were resolved upon by God from ancient times. God has allowed them to arise (v. 25). Here again, then, we have two aspects. God has determined that men should have this power. He has prepared it from of old. He has

173

ordained it long ago. In other words, the military domination of the Assyrian, like the domination of the world by technics and the like, is the result of a divine resolve. Nevertheless, we should recall what we have said previously. God's resolve is not put into effect through man as a robot or object. Man retains his power of decision and his independence even in God's own plan. How can man finally accomplish the plan of God? How can what God prepared long ago be put into effect in the present? The political power of Assyria was ordained, but it is now effected through hatred, butchery, and terror. This is where we see the divine permission. In order that his end may be attained God allows man to use terrible means, means which man himself freely chooses and employs. "I have let you turn fortified cities into heaps of ruins. . . ." But again we find the same lesson that this is not necessarily right in God's eyes. Although what God ordained from of old is accomplished, the way which man chooses is not necessarily good on that account. Man was beautiful and beloved and intelligent, he set a seal on perfection, and God had prepared a great destiny for him . . . but at each period in history, in relation to Sennacherib or to the politicians and technicians of our own time, we can still say and hear again what God says through Ezekiel to the prince of Tyre (Ezekiel 28:1ff.). Everything has been perverted by the means which this perfect one has chosen to actualize the wisdom, beauty, and greatness that God has given him.

Now the crucial point in the choice is not ultimately the selection of this or that means but simply and solely the choice between autonomy and subordination. "Against whom have you raised your voice?" (v. 22). "You have raged against me and your arrogance has come into my ears" (v. 28). Let us make haste to set aside a misunderstanding. Superficially one might take this to mean that while a permissive God is indifferent to the fact that the

Assyrian has massacred men and ruled by war, he is angry the moment the Assyrian mocks and reviles him. Only when he himself is affected does this jealous and inhuman God decide on punishment. This is not at all the meaning of the text, for precisely if the conqueror were to realize that he is in the hands of God and has received his power from him, he could not use all the means which God might permit. He could not butcher men or regard them as mere things. The technician could not despoil nature as he does today. The savant could not be so bent on unraveling all the secrets of the world. The politician could not aim at creating a nationalistic or totalitarian state.

God permits Dionysiac madness and Babel enterprises because he respects man's freedom and these frenzied methods fall within the perspective of his own design. But he also judges them, and he smashes them suddenly at what he takes to be the right time. The problem is that if man would see God's intention in his own action he could no longer follow the pattern of Babel, or Dionysus, or Prometheus. This is why the accusation refers to the attack on God the Lord rather than the millions of victims or the pollution of nature or intellectual madness. For this is the root of the wrong attitude of man. This is the nub or key or cause of the whole business. It is on this that God judges because the rest follows necessarily. If man does not see that the field of his action is given or opened up to him by God, what he does will be bad, exorbitant, and destructive. If he does see it, he makes his choice, which is his real responsibility, according to the insight that all that God permits is not actually possible within the sphere of the right and truth of God. And we must always bear in mind that God is not indifferent to the victims, for ultimately all the victims are *the* Victim, God's own Son, and when God condemns by reason of the offense against his will and love and majesty, this is not an abstract, philosophical, or theoretical declaration. It is in relation to the wars, the social injustices, the exploitation of the poor, and the massacres, that God speaks of this attack upon what he himself is. It is also in relation to the oppression of his people Israel and the church. In other words, God poses in a political context the choice which man must make between recognizing the Lord's sovereignty or not. In the last resort the social (political, economic, or technical) act is the most eloquent manifestation of man's arrogant attempt to dominate God. This is his crowning audacity, far more presumptuous than the verbal audacities of the philosopher or the poet.

When, therefore, God passes his judgment, it is on the occasion of this social choice, but at the level of its deepest motive (the attitude to God) and not the more superficial and secondary ethical motive. Sennacherib is not condemned because he has massacred thousands of people; he has massacred these thousands because he has been a law to himself, regarding himself as independent of God and accountable to nobody. This is why God calls him to account. "Whom have you finally insulted?" We are now in the presence of a mystery. "Have you not perceived that I determined these things long ago?" The term used is a remarkable one. The reference is not to the kind of natural knowledge any man may have. Sennacherib could not know in his heart and conscience that Yahweh is the Lord. He could not discover this in the myths and rites of his religion, nor in the spontaneous respect of religious feeling. On the contrary, the only possible attitude at the natural religious level is that of Rabshakeh, who identifies the Lord with the gods of the defeated nations. What we read is: "Have you not heard?" Have you not found out something you did not know of yourself, something different from what you knew previously, just as one learns a lesson by first of all hearing? This lesson might have been the direct preaching of Jonah to Nineveh if one accepts the historicity of the story, or the older preaching of Amos and Hosea as they proclaimed to the people of God that it would be punished by this savage nation from the north, or the contemporary preaching of Micah and Isaiah, or the most recent warning that the king ought to have understood. These are questions which the historian might ask. How could the conqueror have heard? But God himself knows that the Assyrian has been duly and properly warned. He has made his choice and now God judges this choice. Face to face with God's Word Sennacherib has decided and he has rejected the Word. But man's decision does not affect the situation in the very least. Sennacherib can say that the Lord is an ordinary and mediocre God like all the gods, but this does not mean that he escapes from God's hand. Modern man can say that God is dead, but this does not affect either God or his purpose nor does it allow modern man any effective autonomy. The Assyrian is in God's hand. "I know your sitting down and your going out and coming in, and your raging against me" (v. 27). No matter what may be the Assyrian's power, there is one who encloses him unceasingly, who knows him unceasingly, who both chooses and rejects him, who is both much more profound than he and also radically different. "I will put my hook in your nose and my bit in your mouth, and I will turn you back on the way by which you came" (v. 28). God will treat the conqueror like a wild beast that is subdued, just as Sennacherib treated those defeated by him. All the power that modern man has gained can manifest itself in the long run only in the fact that God will use this very power against the man who hopes to dethrone God. God will use the very means of which man is so proud to subdue this man and reduce him to final destitution.

The judgment is followed by a consolation addressed to Israel in another tone and a different form. The prophet gives a sign. The sign, though remarkable, is not miraculous. Isaiah does not announce the miracle which is to follow. The sign is a set of circumstances by which the king may come to see that the word of Isaiah is true. Like bread and water, this sign is an ordinary one which simply bears witness to the truth of the word which has been spoken to the Assyrian and which is God's Word. This very simple sign is that life will be back to normal in two years. Twice the Assyrian invasion will prevent the farmers from sowing (v. 29), but the third year they will sow afresh and will gather in the harvest. This sign is a guarantee that there is a limit to the power of man and to the exploitation of man, as there is a limit to the chastisement of God.

How simple and vital is this sign! The first year the war comes, harvest is in train, it is halted, and all that can be done is to gather what falls when it is ripe. The second year there is neither sowing nor harvest; only what grows of itself is available. But the third year there will be both sowing and harvest. "You will sow and you will eat the fruit of your labors."

This is in fact a prophecy which often occurs in the prophets. Here again it is given as a sign to Israel, the sign that God is always its God, the Liberator. What? So simple a thing as sowing and reaping? There is nothing miraculous about this. How then can it be a sign? In our eyes it is simply a return to normalcy. For to us things are normal when they are going well. Health, affluence, peace—these are normal, so convinced are we of our own righteousness, of what is our due. But Scripture teaches the very opposite. Unfortunately what is normal now that man is separated from God is war and murder, famine and pollution, accident and disruption. When there is a momentary break in the course of these disasters, when abundance is known, when peace timidly establishes itself, when justice reigns for a span, then it is fitting, unless we are men of too little faith, that we should marvel and give thanks for so great a miracle, realizing that no less than the love and faithfulness of the Lord has been needed in order that there might be this privileged instant. We should tremble for joy as before the new and fragile life of a little child. We should press on with all our force along the way that God has opened up for us. We should see in this "normal" state of life the same thing as the declaration of Jesus Christ, the blind seeing again, the deaf hearing, lepers cleansed. A return to what we regard as normal! But we have no understanding of anything if we think that this is normal, that we have achieved it ourselves, that we deserve it. From this very moment we are engaged in destroying this peace and justice and affluence. From this very moment everything is compromised, and our only option, when things go well, is to see therein the loving grace of the Lord, the sign which is given to us and which also claims us, the sign of the grace shown to us.

The consolation addressed to Hezekiah certainly relates to the end of the siege but only as a kind of accessory conclusion, the real point being the renewing of the covenant between the Lord and his people under the rubric of "the remnant." "And the surviving remnant of the house of Judah shall again take root downward, and shall bear fruit upward; for out of Jerusalem shall go forth a remnant . . . " (vv. 30-31). No matter how great may be God's anger with his people, he will never abandon the people he has chosen; a remnant is promised. There are still members of the covenant people in Judah and the remnant cannot be destroyed, no matter how mighty the powers of the world may be. It is perhaps important to recall this at a time when the church is declining and afraid. For the church has the promise that the gates of hell shall not prevail against it (Matthew 16:18). Irrespective of its defeats, its dechristianization, its infidelity, its inner injustice and outer weakness, the church is still the body of Christ in an ultimate and inalterable way, and there will be a remnant which pushes down roots and produces fruit, even though it consist only of two or three meeting in secret.

But Israel should know, and so too should the church, that this is not in virtue of any righteousness of its own. "For I will defend this city to save it, for my own sake and for the sake of my servant David" (v. 34). Not even for the sake of the love of Hezekiah, although he was a righteous and pious king, a reformer, loyal, obedient, and believing. This puts us in our proper place. Hezekiah profits from God's love, but he cannot embody it, nor replace it, nor carry it to others. If Jerusalem is saved, it is not because of his faith. It is because of God's love for him. If the man to whom we bear witness is saved, it is neither by encounter with us, nor by our words, nor because of our self-giving, but because God has chosen to love man as the expression of his self-love. "For my own sake!" Because God gives himself to his creature, because the love of God for God includes the creature, because God invests the creature with himself. And all this is done in Jesus Christ, not because Jesus has succeeded in emptying himself by some asceticism but because God has divested himself of God for love of himself. All this is done in Jesus Christ, in him alone, and in none other; we cannot pretend either to imitate him or to reproduce him. We can only profit by what is done totally and definitively and once for all. Jerusalem is saved, Jerusalem but not the Assyrian. There must be no confusion at this point. God has not sworn any fidelity to a conquering people. He has chosen it as a scourge, as an executioner, but not as the agent of his love, even though he also encloses it in his love. Here is the whole difference between the church and the world.

The miracle now comes. Pestilence strikes the Assyrian army and it is almost annihilated. The king returns to Nineveh, and after a time he is assassinated by his own sons while prostrated before one of his gods (Nisroch? it should be noted that nothing is known of this god; perhaps it is a faulty transcription of Nusku or Narduk, or possibly a play on words). While we need not stress the point, the historicity of the two events should be observed. According to an Egyptian tradition an invasion of rats caused the flight and death of the Assyrians. Now we know that antiquity was already aware of the relation between rats and plague. It is also true that in 681 B.C. Sennacherib was slain by two of his sons. We need not draw any conclusions as to the accuracy of prophecy, since we have said already that prophecy is not primarily prediction. We may simply remark that the chronicler was not badly informed historically. But this is not the important point. Our stress must be on the fact that the Assyrian did not enter Jerusalem. The limit of his power had indeed been set. The judgment was fulfilled. Furthermore there is a hit at the Assyrian god. It was in his temple, prostrated before him, that Sennacherib was assassinated. This is the reply to the statement that Yahweh is an idol like others, made by men and unable to protect them against the Assyrian. In fact it is the Assyrian god who is unable to protect his worshiper and king. This simple subordinate clause is God's decision in relation to false gods. Finally, it is important to note that for almost the first time in this series of stories a miracle takes place with no help from man at all. This miracle does not come by way of man. It is from heaven. An army is shattered—and all the king does is to pray and all the prophet does is to speak. As noted, this is an exceptional case. At issue here is more than the war, more than the survival of Judah, more than the liberation of Jerusalem. At issue is God's honor. We observe that the miracle of God corresponds to the direct insult addressed by man to God. We ourselves need not seek means to avenge God's honor. God alone avenges his honor. We should simply bow in fear and trembling before this incomprehensible expression of the dignity of his love.

III

But this raises the specific problem of the intervention of miracle in history. The problem is not that of the

Christian or biblical view of history. We shall studiously avoid that here. Our concern is with a particular point. We must dare to take human history as it is without changing its substance or interpreting it as we fancy or throwing a Christian mantle over the concrete facts. There are certainly causalities and correlations in history. The historian is not at fault in trying to find an explanation in previous events. There are economic and political causes for a war and sociological causes for a political regime. Institutions stand in relation to economic, demographic, and ideological phenomena. To be sure, the more facts we know, the harder it is to establish causalities and the more obscure they are. But it is on this horizontal level that we must tackle the question.

Above all we must not try to push God into the system, whether by making him the cause of causes or by establishing a hierarchy in causality. Human causes are adequate, but they do not give events either meaning or direction. A second element has to enter in, and in spite of hostile prejudices we should like to call it ordination or even fatality. Our point is that there is a kind of logic discernible in the evolution of a society or of institutions and events. There are significant and intractable regularities. There are social and economic laws (though we do not give this word the more precise sense it might have in physics). There are irresistible developments in historical processes. Men may do the impossible and yet they cannot halt the course of things or arrest the implacable march of events. Institutions have a weight of their own which causes them to go where men sometimes do not want them to go. There are instances of ineluctable declension. Here, then, are some of the many aspects of what we have called fatality in history. And often those whom we call great men are simply a personal expression of historical fatality. We have the impression that they make history when history would have been more or less the same without

182

them so long as we do not identify the whole of history with the most detailed or superficial event. Yet this fatality is not always the same. There is no all-embracing "Weltgeist" nor exhaustive dialectical explanation. Nor does this fatality affect all men in the same way. Kautsky was right when he showed that at certain points the movement of history is irresistible no matter what may be the intentions or efforts of man, while at others man has a limited possibility of modifying, bending, arresting, or dividing the course of events. Finally, in this sketch of the constituents of history so far as a lay eye can see it, there is indisputably an element of progress, at least in the sense of an evolution or acquired accumulation of instruments, institutions, and sensibilities, if not in the sense of moral or, in the true sense, intellectual progress. It seems as though there is a kind of movement towards the amelioration of man's condition or situation. This progress must be taken seriously even though we should not ascribe infinite value or attribute intrinsic significance to it. This progress is no guarantee at all that history is progress. There may be such long periods of regression that inevitably visions of catastrophe arise. It is no surprise that the period from the fourth to the ninth century should give birth to the pathology of A.D. 1000. The idea that history is progress can be held only by a generation which lives in a society in which there have been some 500 years of accumulated advance. The incontestable fact of progress explains the positive judgment we can have on history, our ideology and our beliefs on the subject. But it does not permit us to affirm that history is progress in itself. Nor does it authorize us to think that progress may be qualitatively understood as the good.

It is in this historical universe and no other that we have to raise the problem of miracle. If we think of God as the Lord of history who inscribes his will directly in our history, then there is no reason for any specific interest in miracle. What we are tempted to call miracle is that which cannot be explained by causality, that which is abnormal compared with the normal flow of things. What seems to suppress the force of events, what disturbs predictable evolution without our knowing why, may sometimes be (except in the cases already mentioned) the man of genius. All economic and sociological explanations dash themselves in vain against the appearance of this kind of gratuitous act for which there are neither roots nor rational explanations. An Alexander or Joan of Arc cannot be explained by any historical rationality. Then there is the mysterious collective fact, whether in direct relation to man or of concern to him. We may mention the sudden disappearance of the bear from caves at a pre-historical time when its development was a direct threat to the existence of the human species. The Arab explosion in 600 and the spread of Marxism between 1880 and 1910 are similar events without either logic or satisfying explanation at the purely human level. History can merely note the facts, go as far as possible in seeking correlations, and then admit that there is an imponderable and strictly independent factor which can neither be grasped nor assimilated and which implies an element of indeterminacy, although there is, of course, no need to see in it the hand of God or to speak of a miracle. In the presence of these phenomena, however, the Christian is obliged to put the problem of their significance for faith and consequently to raise the question of miracles, though he must be careful not to see in this an explanation, nor to press it on non-Christians, nor to think it entitles him to make of it a piece of apologetic. Miracles exist for faith, and God adopts this manner of speaking for those who believe.

Reciprocally the Bible teaches us in effect that God intervenes in the course of events. But, as we have frequently noted, he seldom does so in an explosive, strange, and incomprehensible way. To be sure, one might say that we have here the basis of the theopolitics of Isaiah. God genuinely inserts himself into the course of politics. He acts at his own level, and for Isaiah miracle is the instrument of this insertion. In each miracle God penetrates into the city. He takes it in hand. He makes himself its Lord. In each miracle he contests the authority of the political power, the political autonomy that man always claims, the independent right of man to make history. In each miracle he gives concrete shape to an epoch of divine sovereignty. He forces man to confront him. God has always the full and perfect freedom to act in this surprising and disruptive fashion, to be the supernatural which shatters the course of the natural, with all due deference to Robinson and the rest. But we must carefully avoid the error of assimilating the incomprehensible fact, which the historian can recognize and circle at once, to the objective intervention of God, as though both were miracles. The incomprehensible fact may be a miracle, but a miracle is first God's act, then God's revelation in the interests of the man on whom he has acted, and finally the discerning of the significance for man of this divine intervention; these are the three elements which constitute a miracle.

It is in this sense that one may say there is no miracle except for faith, although absolutely not in the Bultmannian sense, and this is not the faith which from the human standpoint sees a miracle in any event. Any historical event may be revealed by God to be his intervention, and the meaning which results therefrom for faith differs from that which man may attribute to the fact. In the destruction of the Assyrian army, for example, the Egyptians find an explanation in an invasion by rats, and legend even adds that the rats ate the strings of the bows and the straps of the harnesses, so that the Assyrians found themselves without equipment and had to leave. A modern person would regard the pestilence as an epidemic, and the fact that it had important historical consequences does not change its character as such. What is presented to us in the story as a typical explosive miracle representative of the irrational in history—the angel of the Lord destroying the Assyrians—may thus be viewed also from a rational angle. The important thing, then, is God's revelation that he himself is at work here. Yet he was also at work in the ravages of Hazael, and we get no impression of a series of irrational facts in this case. Now we must always bear in mind that the nub of the problem of miracles is to be found in the condemnation and death of Jesus Christ on the cross (more so than in the resurrection, which is radically outside all categories, even that of miracle). We have here a historical event. It took place and can be dated. Jesus Christ was condemned and put to death. In itself this amounts to no more than the death of Spartacus. But the miracle is that he who died on the cross is God himself; he is strictly God intervening in human history, in time, and in the history of each individual. The miracle is that God enters into the life of man even to the point of this death. All other miracles receive their significance from this. And moving on to the relation between a naturalistic view of history and the intervention of the Wholly Other, we may say that the miracle is, in Jesus Christ, that which excludes natural causalities (not for themselves; this is not in itself the miracle) by breaking historical fatality. This is the meaning of the death of Jesus Christ at the intersection of history. It is the incarnation of the Word, and the death of the Incarnate, which interrupts the process of fatality. Here is the authentic event that takes place once for all and can never be reproduced. There is no other authentic event after this one, dated and known. It is quite improper to think that the event can begin again in each of our lives. There is only a contemporaneity which the Spirit ascribes to our actual life as it is carried back to this moment when historical fatality was broken. And it is the fact that God had to die which shows us the gravity and depth and pressure of the fatality. Yet we must not interpret the fact of this unique event as a separation of time into two periods, the one enslaved to fatality, the other free. For all the miracles before Jesus Christ, all the divine interventions in the normal course of history, all the liberations granted by God, find their true point and orientation and weight in the miracle of Jesus Christ. If we return to our previous analysis of the three elements in miracle, Jesus Christ brings the third element into everything that took place prior to him.

Again, subsequent to the great shattering of fatality, the point is not that fatality in the sense used has been annulled or effaced, so that every man is now confronted by a blank page on which he may write without any condition or constraint. Necessity still obtains in the course of history. The historical context cannot be blotted out. There is no intrinsic victory of freedom in history. The death of Jesus Christ does not mean that a strange power which has conditioned history thus far has been annihilated. History and society are still very much subject to constraints. But the breaking of the chain of constraints by the cross has incalculable historical consequences. It is the white horse which goes through the world with the three others and intermingles its action with theirs. Historical forces are, as it were, unceasingly repairing the web of necessity, and in different forms the web is being broken, annulled, and disrupted afresh by the action of the power of freedom unleashed at the cross. For Jesus Christ has set in motion the power of freedom, and he has done this very concretely in the course of history, though this does not mean that history has become a kind of triumphal march, stage by stage, of victories for freedom. Our own age shows the very opposite. What has been done and gained is that a man or men can now acquire the power of freedom, and by them miracles may be done in history.

There is no generality or necessity about this. It is not

certain that men will perform these miracles. They are under no constraint. Nor is it necessary that it should be Christians who perform them. The door is open to man, and man may enter. When he makes this decision, when he undertakes the tremendous risk of reintroducing freedom into the course of history, then, whether he knows it or not, he has with him all the power of God, the power destroyed at the cross, but the power which is historical because it has willed to spill over into history like a dead body giving fertility to the earth. This man now changes the profound reality of history even though he is not a great man, a general, or a politician, and even though the apparent event of economic crisis or military victory or stability of government is in no way altered. He changes the profound reality of history because it is no longer a mechanism. He slips a new factor into the totality of pieces, causes, and factors. Conversely, when a man will not accept this power, the aggressiveness of necessity becomes more total and stifling. The power of miracles which has been set in the course of history by Jesus Christ is not a neutral power subject to man's control. The Word of God itself is a power of life or a power of death. In history, too, there is the chance of miracle or of disaster and collapse. This is already written in filigree in the series of stories from Second Kings on which we have been meditating. If man grasps this grace and freedom he fulfils both his own being and also God's design, for God writes his design in this freedom which man assumes and which forces destiny. This is miracle. But if man neglects this divine power for freedom, the miracle accomplished in Jesus Christ, then he may do many important things in history, but only within the framework of necessity and by the force of things. In truth the freedom of man attained in Jesus Christ is what really makes history. The crowds who obey sociological or economic laws do not make history; they repeat it. The freedom of man is a miraculous phenomenon which is decisive for history. When men express freedom, they are witnesses to the act of the Creator God in history.

But there are other men who alone present the true meaning of history; these are the prophets. These two kinds of free men are the miracle of God. What, then, is the meaning of this miracle? If we are to judge by the miracles which God did in the course of Old Testament history, and which all express the love of God in freedom, history is by nature a combination of forces, and always tends to reproduce constraints and to establish the bondage of man under one form or another. At every stage it finally results in an intolerable situation. Hence it has constantly to be called in question both as history and also as result or situation. There has to be reintroduced into it the truth of freedom so that one part of the reality of history itself may be upheld and man may enjoy and express his autonomy and bring forth its fruits, but so that the other part too may move towards the final goal which God has marked out for it. The first element reminds us that if the reality of man's action is not respected we shall finish up with "nonhistory," with a kind of nontemporal installation such as, e.g., the attainment of the communist city, or, indeed, what is implied by a theocratic interpretation of history.

The second element reminds us that God fixes an orientation to history and that the truth of this is the free fulfilment of his plan and purpose. Miracle comes in at the minor level, as here in the liberation of Jerusalem, which serves to attest God's love for it and to grant it a breathing-space. But the miracle in Jesus Christ implies that henceforth the goal of history can be attained by the deliberate act of man responding to the love of God by way of the cross.

Meditation on Inutility

In spite of God's respect and love for man, in spite of God's extreme humility in entering into man's projects in order that man may finally enter into his own design, in the long run one cannot but be seized by a profound sense of the inutility and vanity of human action. To what end is all this agitation, to what end these constant wars and states and empires, to what end the great march of the people of Israel, to what end the trivial daily round of the church, when in the long run the goal will inevitably be attained, when it is always ultimately God's will that is done, when the most basic thing of all is already achieved and already attained in Jesus Christ? One can understand the scandalized refusal of modern man who can neither accept the inutility of what he has done nor acquiesce in this overruling of his destiny. One can understand that the man who wants to be and declares himself to be of age is unwilling to acknowledge any tutor, and, when he surveys the giddy progress of his science, cannot admit that it has all been already accomplished by an incomprehensible decree of what he can only regard as another aspect of fatality. In fact, in spite of all that we have been able to learn in these pages, before God we are constantly seized by an extreme feeling of inutility. It begins already on the sixth day, when we come up against the inutility of the

190

function of Adam in the garden of Eden. Here is this man, the lord and master of a creation which has been handed over to him and which is perfect when set under the eye of God. Yahweh takes man and sets him in the garden of Eden in order that he may till it and keep it. But what sense is there in tilling it? Already on the third day God has set up the order whereby plants and trees propagate themselves. Everything grows in abundance. God himself causes trees of all kinds to grow out of the soil and they are pleasant to the sight and good for food. What can tilling mean in these conditions? The point of tilling is either that things cannot grow without it, or that the various species should be improved, or that plants which produce food should be protected against noxious weeds, or that the yield should be increased. But in this perfect order there is no place for cultivation. And keeping? Against whom or what is man to keep it? What external enemy threatens the perfect work in which everything is good? What protection can man give to a world where God himself is the full protector? Against what disorder is he to keep it when order is the finished work of God? What place is there for tilling and keeping in the perfect fellowship and unity represented by God's work, in this creation in which there is no division, when everything has a part in everything else, when each fragment is not just a fragment united to all the others but also an expression of the total unity of a creation that reflects the perfection of its creator, when the bond between the Lord and the universe is of such perfection that the Lord's rest is the equilibrium of his creation? Tilling and keeping make sense only in a world in which things are divided, the unity is shattered, equilibrium has been disturbed, and the relation between the Lord and his creature has been destroyed. To till it and keep it? It is God's command and yet a useless service.

Then we are confronted by the law or will of God broken down into commandments entailing our works.

But works to what end? What are we to make of the long struggle of the Hebrew people, which regards works as necessary to salvation, except that it is all useless? What are we to make of works performed to effect reconciliation with God, except that they are all in vain? The whole frenzied effort of well-intentioned man has been crushed. At a stroke we learn that in Jesus Christ salvation is given to us, that God loved us first before we did anything, that all is grace; grace—gracious gift, free gift. Life and salvation, resurrection and faith itself, glory and virtue, all is grace, all is attained already, all is done already, and even our good works which we strive with great difficulty to perform have been prepared in advance that we should do them. It is all finished. We have nothing to achieve, nothing to win, nothing to provide. On this road it is not that half is done by God and half by man. The whole road has been made by God, who came to find man in a situation from which he could not extricate himself. But what about works? Not just the deadly works of the law, which are deadly because man thinks he can fashion his own salvation, which is his destiny, by them, but the works of faith, the works without which faith itself is dead, the works which are the expression of the new birth, the fruits of the Spirit—of what use are these works? Why should we do them? Here again we come up against the same inutility, the same vanity, as we contemplate God's omniprescience and stand in the perfect presence of his love. And yet works are demanded of us; they are God's command and yet a useless service.

We turn next to prayer, to the relation with the Father which Jesus himself taught, the gift which confuses us since what is given to us is that we may speak with God as a man speaks with his friend. But again the thought arises: Your Father knows what you need. Of what use is it, then, to confide our fears and plans to him, to present our requests and problems? God knows well in advance that we are not aware of all our needs, of all that saddens us, of all that lacerates us. He knows in advance. What good is it, then, to seek his blessing, his help, the gift of his Spirit? What good is it to pray to him for our mutual salvation and to present to his love the living and the dead? Does he not know them each one? For each one did he not on Calvary undergo the shed blood and the bowed head? For each one has he not decided in love from all eternity and brought his benediction in person to all distress and toil? And when we haltingly seek to express ourselves in prayer, we have every reason to be discouraged in advance: "You do not know yourselves what you should ask." You do not know your true needs or real good. Fortunately there is one to help. The Holy Spirit intercedes for you before the Father with sighs that cannot be uttered (Romans 8:26ff.). But if this perfect prayer is rendered by other lips than ours, if it is out of our hands, of what avail is our own awkward formulation of our requests and complaints? Why put our hands together for him who himself prays for us? We are thus struck by the vanity of prayer, by its inadequacy and poverty. Prayer? It is God's command and yet a useless service.

Then there is wisdom, human wisdom, man's intelligent ordering of his life, the serious employment of right reason, the attempt to find the proper way of life, the whole enterprise that takes form in political action and personal morality, in social work and poetry, in economic management and the building of temples, in the constant improvement of justice by changing laws, in philosophy and technology, the manifold wisdom of man which is also inscribed in the wisdom of God and which may be an expression of this wisdom, the first of all God's works that rejoiced before him when he laid the foundations of the world (Proverbs 8:22ff.). And yet—are we not told that God has convicted of folly the wisdom of the world? "For the foolishness of God is wiser than the wisdom of men. . . . Consider your call, brethren; not many of you were wise according to worldly standards" (1 Corinthians 1:18ff.). Human wisdom, futile pride, a Babel built by those who think they are wiser than God; man has been able to plumb the depths, to find gold there, and to explore the oceans, as Job says, "but where shall wisdom be found?" (Job 28). Human wisdom, an incomparable excuse for all that we are not, under the concealment of all that we do! But should we invent it? Should we reject all its work? Should we lead the world to nothingness, because nothingness is the way of resurrection? Should we already cut the harvest because the venomous fruits of wisdom are indissolubly linked to the adorable fruits of the same reason? It is not yet time, says Jesus, and he restrains the seventh angel; wisdom must pursue its work. Wisdom; it is the command of God and yet a useless service.

We now come to preaching. What language, what word, what image, what eloquence can pass on a little of this flame to others? All that we count most dear and profound and true, we want to communicate, not to make others like ourselves, not to win them or constrain them, but to show them the way of life, the irreplaceable way of love which has been given to us, so that they can have a share in the joy of this wedding. But the language is empty and conveys nothing; the form gives evidence of our own unskillful hands. Nothing becomes true except by the Holy Spirit. What can we say, and why should we say it, if everything depends on this unpredictable act of the Spirit of God who blows where he wills (John 3:8) and lays hold of whom he wills, if inward illumination is directly from God, who calls Paul when he is a persecutor and Augustine in his rhetorical pursuits and makes all truth known to both of them? If our words to even the dearest of brothers are lifeless and fall to the ground unless the Holy Spirit comes and breathes on them, if our tongue is mute in spite of our illusions, as that of Zechariah was (Luke 1:19ff.), or if, which is worse, it is unclean, as that of Isaiah was (Isaiah 6:5), and if the angel alone can release it, what is the good of preaching and speaking and witnessing and evangelizing? Does not God do it quite well by himself? And yet—"How are they to believe in him of whom they have never heard? And how are they to hear without a preacher? ... So faith comes from what is heard ... " (Romans 10:14-17), and again: "Go ... teach all nations" (Matthew 28:19). Futile preaching, and yet so important that Paul can cry: "Woe to me if I do not preach the gospel" (1 Corinthians 9:16). Preaching! It is God's command and yet it is useless service.

What we have been saying can all be summed up in the judgment which Jesus passes with intolerable clarity: "Say, 'We are unworthy servants.' " But we should isolate two different elements in this saying in Luke 17:10. Jesus says: "When you have done all that is commanded. . . ." Jesus is not evading the problem of law and order. There is a divine law, which is a commandment, and which is addressed to us. Hence we have to fulfil it to the letter. We have to do all that is commanded. The sense or conviction of the utter futility of the work we do must not prevent us from doing it. The judgment of uselessness is no excuse for inaction. It is not before doing or praying or preaching that we are to proclaim their inutility. It is not before their work that Elisha, Jehu, and Hezekiah proclaim the uselessness of their work, which is only a fulfilment of God's action. Pronounced in advance, futility becomes justification of scorn of God and his word and work. It is after doing what is commanded, when everything has been done in the sphere of human decisions and means, when in terms of the relation to God every effort has been made to know the will of God and to obey it, when in the arena of life there has been full acceptance of all responsibilities and interpretations and commitments and conflicts, it is then and only then that the judgment takes on meaning: all this (that we had to do) is useless; all this we cast from us to put it in thy hands, O Lord; all this belongs no more to the human order but to the order of thy kingdom. Thou mayest use this or that work to build up the kingdom thou art preparing. In thy liberty thou mayest make as barren as the fig-tree any of the works which we have undertaken to thy glory. This is no longer our concern. It is no longer in our hands. What belonged to our sphere we have done. Now, O Lord, we may set it aside, having done all that was commanded. This is how Elisha and Elijah finished their course.

The second point to be noted in the verse is that it is not God or Jesus who passes the verdict of inutility. It is we ourselves who must pronounce it on our work: "We are unprofitable servants." God does not judge us thus. He does not reject either us or our works. Or rather, he does not echo the verdict if we have passed it ourselves. If (as Christ demands) we judge ourselves in this way when we have done all we could do and accepted all our responsibilities, if we are able to view our own works and most enthusiastic enterprises with the distance and detachment and humor that enable us to pronounce them useless, then we may be assured of hearing God say: "Well done, good and faithful servant" (Matthew 25:21). But if we pass in advance this bitter judgment of uselessness that paralyzes and discourages us, if we are thus completely lacking in love for God, or if on the other hand we magnify our works and regard them as important and successful (Jesus, little Jesus, I have so wonderfully exalted you, but if I had attacked you in your defenselessness your shame would have been as great as your glory. . . .), if we come before God decked out in the glory of these lofty, grandiose, and successful works, then . . . "Woe to you that are rich" (Luke 6:24), for the rich man today is the successful man.

Everything is useless, and we are thus tempted to add:

Everything, then, is vanity. We are tempted, for it is a temptation to do only what is useful and to assimilate the judgment of Ecclesiastes on vanity (1:2ff.) to the inutility which we have been briefly sketching. Now this spontaneous reaction raises a question. Why are we so concerned about utility? Why do we regard what is not useful as worthless? In reality, we are obsessed at this point by the views of our age and century and technology. Everything has to serve some purpose. If it does not, it is not worth doing. And when we talk in this way we are not governed by a desire to serve but by visions of what is great and powerful and effective. We are driven by the utility of the world and the importance of results. What counts is what may be seen, achievement, victory, whether it be over hunger or a political foe or what have you. What matters is that it be useful.

My desire in these meditations on the Second Book of Kings is to call our judgments into question. Yes, prayer is useless, and so too are miracles and theology and the diaconate and works and politics. The healing of Naaman served no purpose, nor did the massacres of Jehu.

The piety of Hezekiah could be no more effective than the impiety of Ahaz. But what then? We must fix our regard on another dimension of these acts, of all these acts that kings and prophets had to perform. It is just because these acts were useless and did not carry with them their own goal and efficacy that they are on the one hand testimonies to grace and on the other an expression of freedom. To be controlled by utility and the pursuit of efficacy is to be subject to the strictest determination of the actual world. To want to attain results is necessarily not to be a witness to the free gift of God. If we are ready to be unworthy or unprofitable servants (although busy and active at the same time), then our works can truly redound to the glory of him who freely loved us first. God loved us because he is love and not to get results. Our works are thus given a point of departure and they are not in pursuit of an objective. If we act, it is because God has loved us, because we have been saved, because God's Spirit dwells in us, because we have received revelation, and not at all in order that we may be saved, or that others may be converted, or that society may become Christian or happy or just or affluent, or that we may overcome hunger or be good politicians. Elisha goes to anoint Hazael because he is ordered to do so and not so that Hazael may do good. In this way the freedom of our acts, released from worry about usefulness or efficacy, can be a parable of the freedom of the love of God; but not in any other way.

It is thus in this bread cast on the waters (Ecclesiastes 11:1), in all these somber and passionate acts we have been reading about together, in all these past decisions, that we have seen outcroppings of freedom. Just because these acts were useless within the plan of God, man was free to do them. But he had to do them. To do a gratuitous, ineffective, and useless act is the first sign of our freedom and perhaps the last. The men of the Second Book of Kings, each in his own place, played their part for God. But none of them was indispensable. None of them served in a decisive way the great plan of the Father accomplished in the Son, the mysterious purpose the angels wanted to look into (1 Peter 1:12). None of them did the radical deed, and each was free in his own way. "A wonderful freedom," one might say, "if it can have only vain and futile works as its object? If to be successful we must be subject to necessity or fatality, then so be it!" In fact, if nothing in the Second Book of Kings had taken place, if none of the decisions of these men had been made, little would have changed. Israel and Judah would have been led into exile, the remnant would still have been weak, and the plan of God would have been fulfilled as it was in Jesus Christ. Nothing would have been different in the facts, in what we call history. If we do not pray, if we do not do the works of faith, if we do not seek after wisdom, if we do not preach the gospel, nothing in history, nor very probably in the church, would look much different. The world would go its way, and the kingdom of God would finally come by way of judgment. And yet there would be lacking something irreplaceable and incommensurable, something that is measured neither by institutions nor metaphysics nor products nor results, something that modifies everything qualitatively and nothing quantitatively, something that gives the only possible meaning to human life, and yet that cannot belong to it, that cannot be its fruit, that is not its nature. This is freedom: man's freedom within God's freedom; man's freedom as a reflection of God's freedom; man's freedom exclusively received in Christ; man's freedom which is free obedience to God and which finds unique expression in childlike acts, in prayer and witness, as we see these in the Second Book of Kings, within the tragic acts of politics and religion.

DATE DUE

DEC 3 1987			
JAN 2 1 1988			